WHAT
EVERY
CHRISTIAN
SHOULD
BELIEVE

WHAT EVERY CHRISTIAN SHOULD BELIEVE

WILLIAM EVANS

MOODY PRESS
CHICAGO

Library of Congress Cataloging-in-Publication Data

Evans, William, 1870-1950
    What every Christian should believe / by William Evans
    p. cm.
    Originally published: Chicago:Bible Institute Colportage
    Association, c1922
    ISBN 0-8024-5220-5
    1. Theology, Doctinal—Popular works. I. Title

BT77 .E85 2001
230—dc21

                                                          00-053314

1 3 5 7 9 10 8 6 4 2
Printed in the United States of America

CONTENTS

NOTE TO OUR READERS

The ultimate impact of any book can be measured by how well the author communicates on a particular subject. The accuracy of the message and its relevance to the reader are also critical elements that distinguish a select group of books from the multitude that are available. Most important, those books that build on the foundation of the Bible, with an overriding goal of glorifying God, are the ones that will be of greatest value to the reader. It is these writings that will stand the test of time.

This group of books, taken from the archives of Moody Press, meets those criteria. They are clear in their presentation and easy to read and apply to your life. At the same time, they do not compromise on substance, while presenting strong arguments that remain relevant to today's readers.

The authors write with elegance and conviction; their passion will inspire you. We have chosen to use the New King James Version of the Bible, which maintains the beauty and grace of the original King James Version while being highly readable in today's language.

This series of books is part of our Life Essentials™ line of products because the books fit so well with Life Essentials' objective: to help the readers stay focused on the essentials of life by keeping God at the center of all they do, grounding them in those truths that build their faith and obedience to the triune God.

We pray that these books will bless and help you in your walk of faith, just as they have done for followers of Jesus Christ in past generations.

THE PUBLISHER

PREFACE

In judging this book, it should be remembered for whom it is particularly prepared. It is for the young believer, the Christian who does not know the simple and yet fundamental doctrines of the Christian faith. It is prepared for men and women who know Christ as a personal Savior by experiential knowledge but have had little or no specific instruction in the leading doctrines of the Christian faith.

Scripture references are quite numerous, because it is our purpose to send readers to their Bibles in order that they may have a "Thus says the Lord" as an anchor for their faith.

Necessarily, the subjects are briefly treated, for this volume is only a primer of Christian doctrine. For an exhaustive study of these and other doctrines composing the Christian faith, see *The Great Doctrines of the Bible*, by the author and published by Moody Press.

It is our earnest wish and prayer that this book will be used in the building up of those who are either young in or ignorant of the things pertaining to the King.

WILLIAM EVANS

INTRODUCTION

KNOWING SOUND DOCTRINE

THE IGNORANCE AMONG CHRISTIANS regarding the fundamental doctrines of their faith is surprisingly great, widespread, and alarming. Definite knowledge and instruction in other and far less important spheres of life are being insisted upon; why not, then, in the highest realm—that of a man's religion?

Ignorance in any sphere of life is calamitous; in religion it is fatal. "My people are destroyed for lack of knowledge" (Hosea 4:6). How disastrous it would be to human life, safety, and happiness if the doctor were as ignorant of his *materia medica*, the druggist of his *pharmacopeia*, or the lawyer and judge of his *statutes*, as the average Christian is of the great and fundamental doctrines of his faith.

Not to know God is to fail to have eternal life (see John 17:3). To be ignorant of those great truths that have to do with spiritual and eternal verities is to miss life's greatest quest: to be at last "forever with the Lord" in "an inexpressible and glorious joy."

Much of the failure in Christian experience comes from ignorance of the great facts of redemption. Romans 6–8 describes the struggle of the soul to gain the mastery over sinful heredity and adverse environment. That ignorance of the great facts of redemption lies at the base of such failure is evident from the recurring phrase found in this connection as used by the apostle: "Do you not know?" It appears in Romans 6:3, 16; 7:1; 11:2 (see also 1 Corinthians 3:16; 5:6; 6:2–3, 9, 15–16, 19; 9:13, 24). Certain great Christian truths have to be *reckoned* on (Romans 6:11) in order to achieve a victorious life. But they must be first known before they can be thus reckoned (see Romans 10:14–17). When a Christian distinctly appreciates his *standing* in Christ, his spiritual state and condition will be greatly affected.

MOVING FROM IGNORANCE
TO KNOWLEDGE

Ignorance of the great truths of our Christian religion has brought gloom, despair, and even suicide to many people. A lady, accompanied by her sister, called on a minister for spiritual aid. The sister was about to be committed to an asylum for the insane. Her gloom and despondence were attributed to spiritual depression. She had decided that she had committed "the sin against the Holy Ghost," that she was "guilty of the unpardonable sin," and that, consequently, there was "no forgiveness" for her, that she was therefore eternally lost. This conclusion had been reached on the basis of her interpretation (rather misinterpretation) of certain parts of the Bible (e.g., Matthew 12:31–32; Hebrews 6:4–6; 10:26–27).

The minister carefully instructed this lady, removed the misinterpretations, and caused her to rightly understand the Scriptures. Within a few weeks the clouded brain became again clear, the gloom passed away, and she was her real self. In a real sense, this woman was perishing for lack of knowledge of the great facts of her salvation.

With greater knowledge in spiritual matters would come correspondingly greater results in Christian service. One is amazed at the great increase in farm products brought about by scientific instruction in the cultivation of the soil. In like manner, greater "fruit of the Spirit" would undoubtedly follow a better and deeper knowledge of the "law of the Spirit of life in Christ Jesus" (Romans 8:2; note Galatians 5:22–23).

Far too many Christians, while spiritually minded, are not scripturally instructed. This is why so many are led away from the truth into the false "isms," by every wind of strange doctrine that blows about them, "by the trickery of men," and by "the cunning craftiness" (Ephesians 4:14) represented by such erroneous sects as Christian Science, spiritualism, and Mormonism. And, is it not a fact that the reason it is so hard to win such people back to the truth is because they become so soon indoctrinated in the erroneous beliefs they have accepted?

See with what avidity the scientist devours Mrs. Eddy's book, *Science and Health;* the Millennial Dawnist, *The Plan of the Ages!* Would that every Christian devoured his Bible in like manner! When such Bible study takes place, when Christians become thus thoroughly indoctrinated in the tenets of their faith, then false cults will die for lack of uninstructed professing Christian material on which they feed and grow.

The Christian must grow in the knowledge of God as in divine grace (2 Peter 3:18). There should be no conflict between the growth in knowledge and faith; in reality none exists. The Scriptures do not make the invidious distinction between believing with the head and the heart so often made nowadays. "How shall they believe in him of whom they have not heard?" (Romans 10:14). Increase in spiritual knowledge and faith should go together (see Romans 10:9–10). Too often our faith is limited by our ignorance. If we knew more, we would doubtless believe more. We trust God as far as we have come to know Him. Unfortunately, He is still to many "the unknown God" (Acts 17:23).

KNOWLEDGE AS THE TRUE
BASIS OF PRACTICE

There is a crying need today of a more intelligent and better understood faith on the part of the followers of Jesus Christ. We do not know God, Christ, the Bible, the Holy Spirit, and the great doctrines of our faith as we should. The early Christian church had men of rare scholarship and goodness to devote their entire time to the definite instruction in Christian doctrine of those who offered themselves for membership in the church. The great pity is that such catechetical instruction has been allowed so largely to pass out of the domain of the church and that so many of the youth of our churches have been deprived of so great a boon.

It is a false and pernicious reasoning that would make belief nothing, and practice everything. No exhortation to a strong, virtuous, and holy life will be able to grip the heart and conscience that does not have behind it the conviction of a great truth. What a man believes or does not believe affects, and very seriously too, his whole conduct. Back of all the exhortations of the apostle Paul to a holy life, a good conscience, and pure living, there will be found a call for a knowledge of and faith in "sound doctrine" (Titus 1:9).

The needs of the age demand men and women with a definite and clearly stated faith, particularly with regard to the fundamentals of Christian belief. It was such a knowledge and persuasion that gave apostolic preaching an authority and power that staggers us and shames our faintly expressed and compromising presentation of the truth. The apostles spoke with authority; today many have lost that sharp focus and positive note that gave those first preachers such wonderful audacity and positiveness in their proclamation of the gospel truths.

SETTLED THINGS

Some things in "the faith which was once for all delivered to the saints" (Jude 3) are definitely and clearly settled. We ought to know what they are and declare them unhesitatingly, fearless as to consequences. We should hew to the line, let the chips fall where they will. The apostle's words "Prove all things" have been greatly misunderstood. Some things in the Christian faith have been settled once for all. They are not in need of any proof save that of experience. They have passed beyond the experimental stage; they now have their place in the realm of certainty. Such certainties formed "the form (or outline) of sound doctrine" of which the apostle speaks in the Pastoral Epistles, and to which he so uncompromisingly demands adherence. Just as in science certain things are assumed and used as a working hypothesis, without which there could be no experimental progress, so it is with the Christian faith: there are certain fundamental doctrines without the knowledge of which there can not very well be any advancement in Christian faith, practice, or service.

In this book we will explore what every Christian should believe about God; the Bible, its power and authority; Jesus, His identity and ministry; the Holy Spirit; and Satan. These are five fundamental and yet vital areas that affect a Christian's faith and practice.

Every Christian, be he a leader or a follower, will find his faith challenged again and again. Therefore, he must be able to give to every person who asks about his faith "a reason for the hope that is in [him]" (1 Peter 3:15). He must be able to say, "Credo!"—I believe!—and state *what* he believes, and *why* he believes it. To aid in this needy and worthy purpose is the aim of this book.

CHAPTER ONE

THE BIBLE:
ITS POWER

THE SUPREME REVELATION of God—far greater than the revelation of Himself in nature, history, or providence—is found in the sacred Scriptures. Without the revelation contained in the Bible, we would be ignorant of God, His nature, will, plans, purpose; of Christ and the great doctrines of our salvation; of the Holy Spirit and His wonderful ministrations towards believers in Christ; and of our future destiny in the great eternity.

At the foundation of all our spiritual knowledge, then, lies the Word of God. The Holy Spirit does not operate apart from this Word.

Far more important to the child of God, in a sense, is the

study of the Scriptures than is prayer. How would we know what to pray for, how to pray acceptably, and to whom to pray if we did not have the written revelation of these things? When we pray, *we* talk to God; when we read and study His Word, *He* talks to us. Which is the more important, think you: that we talk to Him, or that He talks to us?

The Christian should know that the Bible will always be spoken against; therefore, he should not fear opposition to the Word. "Forever, O Lord, Your word is settled in heaven" (Psalm 119:89).

The Bible, even as the Christ, has been and ever will be "a stone of stumbling and a rock of offense"; that on which "many . . . shall stumble; they shall fall and be broken, be snared and taken" (Isaiah 8:14–15). There is no more fiercely attacked book than the Bible—attacked by both friends and foes. It may be said that today the Bible is actually suffering more from the attacks made upon it by its professed friends than from all the machinations of its enemies. The destructive high criticism which has done so much to destroy faith in the supernatural revelation found in the Scriptures will have much to answer for in the great day of reckoning.

The faith of the Christian should not be shaken because of these attacks. God has told us not to be disturbed over them. He says: "Behold, I lay in Zion a stone for a foundation, a tried stone, a precious cornerstone, a sure foundation; whoever believes will not act hastily" (Isaiah 28:16). These words are true of the incarnate and written Word alike. The words "whoever believes will not act hastily" mean that the person who puts confidence in the Word "shall not be put to shame or confusion at such a time." The Christian need not worry when he sees the Bible being attacked. It is "an anvil that has worn out many hammers."

THE ALWAYS-ABIDING WORD OF GOD

God has forewarned us to expect that some builders will refuse to build upon this stone, and that they will scorn it and cast it aside. But He also assures us that the stone will remain unshaken. The Word of God will abide even though heaven and earth pass away (see Matthew 5:18).

During earlier centuries, forms of opposition to the Word of God were much more severe than those that characterize the criticism in our day. One has only to think back to that dark period at the birth of Christianity when its Founder lay dead in that tomb in Joseph's garden. Surely no enterprise ever seemed more hopeless or so completely at an end. Yet forth from the shadow of that cross and tomb there went a band of men to proclaim the truths contained in the Bible, and that with glorious victory and unprecedented success.

Or, again, one has only to look back upon those

gloomy days when the apostle Paul, the champion, the leader, the foremost representative of Christianity, lay languishing in the Roman prison, his head about to be laid upon the executioner's block, in order to realize in what straits the religion of Christ then found itself. Yet it survived even that shock.

The student of history has but to think of those fierce days of opposition from paganism with its gross sensuality; of oriental philosophy, with its keen logic and reason; of the Renaissance of the fifteenth century, with its worship of reason and attempted dethronement of faith, to understand that if the Bible had not been a divine book it would have been destroyed centuries ago.

So dire was the condition of Christianity in England in the eighteenth century that Bishop Butler in his "Advertisement" to his *Analogy of Religion* wrote: "It has come, I know not how, to be taken for granted by many persons that Christianity is not so much a subject for inquiry; but that it is now, at length, discovered to be fictitious; and accordingly they treat it as if, in the present age, this were an agreed point among all people of discernment, and nothing remained but to set it up as a principal subject of mirth and ridicule." Can the greatest pessimist amongst us say that Christianity is in anything like such a condition today?

Voltaire said that in one hundred years from his day, the Bible would be an unknown book; that if a man wanted to find it he would have to go to some antiquarian bookstore, and there, on some back shelf, he might, perhaps, find a copy of the Bible. Over one hundred years have passed since Voltaire made this statement, and it does not look as though it were anywhere near being fulfilled, for the Bible today is a more popular book than ever before in all its history. We venture to say that the theological controversies raging around the Bible today are nothing but a rehash of those of the past centuries, served up in new dress, as a comparison will show.

The Bible withstood the shocks of those days, and why should it not withstand the same shocks today? In spite of all opposition, the church of Christ today has more members, builds more churches, circulates more Bibles, and makes her influence felt all over the world more than ever in all her previous history.

THE OFTEN-ACKNOWLEDGED
WORD OF GOD

We should not, therefore, fear that Christianity and the Bible are going to pieces because it is asserted that the *scholars* of the day are against it. Of course, it is not true that the scholars of the world are arrayed against the Bible. Professor Tait of Edinburgh, a distinguished representative of physical science, denied such a statement in the *International Review*. He asked who were the *advanced, best, ablest* thinkers of the past, or of that time. He then showed that, with a few ex-

23

ceptions, the scholars were on the side of the Bible and orthodoxy. The late George C. Romanes, who, after a long eclipse of the faith, died a believer, in addressing the students of Cambridge University, said that all the most illustrious names were listed on the side of orthodoxy: Sir. W. Thompson, Sir George Stokes, Professors Tait, Adams, Clark, Maxwell, and Bailey—and the conditions are practically unchanged today.

But if it were true that scholarship is arrayed against the Bible, that fact would not predict or spell defeat or failure. Scholarship has never saved the church or brought it back from its backslidings to warmth or spiritual fervor. Philosophy and science never have nor never can save a soul. We are saved by faith, not by scholarship. Jesus Christ did not choose a company of university men to be His disciples and apostles, to go forth and win the world for God. We are not disparaging scholarship; we need it, and the more consecrated scholarship we have, the better for the interests of the Bible and Christianity. No premium should be put upon ignorance. The principal authors of the Old and New Testaments, Moses and Paul, were scholars. What we do assert is that Christianity is not dependent upon scholarship (1 Corinthians 1:24–26).

We need not fear the increase in the knowledge of the sciences. Voltaire said that the Bible would not survive a century after the law of gravitation had been discovered. Yet we know that the discoverer of that law, Sir Isaac Newton, was a humble Christian man; and Christianity still survives, even though the law of gravitation is an acknowledged scientific fact. Strauss, the skeptic, maintained that the Copernican system would give the deathblow to Christianity and the Bible; who is there today who feels that his faith in Christianity is even shaken because he believes that the earth revolves around the sun, and not, as the ancients believed, the opposite? The Bible has nothing to fear from the pickax of the geologist, from the telescope of the astronomer, from the skull of the anthropologist, from the instrument of the chemist, or from the pen of the scientific writer.

Every Christian should know how to approach the Bible.
"Open my eyes, that I may see wondrous things from Your law" (Psalms 119:18).

How should each Christian approach the Bible? *First, the approach should be a personal one.* He should read and study the Bible firsthand, and for himself. He should be more anxious to hear what the Spirit will teach him, through prayerful waiting, what the Word of God actually says, than what writers and commentators have to say about what it says, or what they think it says, or, as is sometimes the case, what it should say. It is better to ask the Bible what it says than to tell it what to say.

Some people study books about nature and call that nature study. The best place to study nature is in the fields and woods. Books and pictures are but reflections of nature. If you want to enjoy the beauty of a garden, you do not send someone else out to look at it for you. You do not study nature by proxy; why then should you study the Word of God by proxy?

We are prone to substitute books and helps for the Word of God. Helps they may be toward the understanding of it, but substitutes for the firsthand study of the Scriptures by the aid of the Holy Spirit they never can be. Let the Bible speak to you for itself. Listen, yourself, to its voice. If it is my health you are discussing, then I have a right to be heard, for I know how I feel better than the doctors or you can tell me. So if the Bible is the issue, then let it speak for itself. Let it give its own account of how it came to be (see 2 Timothy 3:16; 2 Peter 1:20–21), and what are the conditions it imposes on those who would understand its teachings (see 1 Corinthians 2:10–16).

Second, the Christian should approach the Bible as a unique Book. "As man is among the animals, so is the Bible among books." It is not a matter of difference with regard to degree, but of intrinsic quality. All other books are human; the Bible is divine. All other books are man-wrought; the Bible is God-breathed. Other books are the products of the human understanding; the Bible is the result of the moving in the hearts of holy men by the Holy Spirit of God. The Bible is not like the books of other religions: they are comparative. The Bible is not in that class; it is superlative.

The Bible is not a book; it is *the* Book. For this reason it is impossible for the Christian to read the Bible "just as he would read any other book," as he is so often told he should do. He cannot do it because the Bible is *not like* other books. Shall a man read a letter from his revered and departed mother just as he would read an advertisement? He simply cannot do it. One can read the Bible as he reads other books only when other books make the same claims that the Bible makes for itself. And even then the rival claimants must be subjected to strictest criticism and judgment.

No other book in fact makes claims such as the Bible makes. Dealing with this subject, the Scottish preacher John McNeill said: "You ask me to look on the Bible as I would on any other book? You might as well ask me to look upon every other woman as I look upon my wife. I simply cannot do it. I won't do it. You may call me narrow and a bigot, and straightlaced, all that, and more too, if you like. But after you have had your say, I must tell you that after I have looked on other women I am powerfully prejudiced in favor of my wife Peggy."

Shakespeare, Milton, Browning, Carlyle, Ruskin, and other noted writers are a literary luxury; the Bible is a vital necessity. They are cake; the Bible is bread. "The words that I speak unto you are spirit, and they are life," said Jesus (John 6:63). He was saying that the

Bible is life-giving and life-sustaining. This cannot be said of any other book in the world. The Christian must recognize this fact in his approach to it. True, it is literature—it is the "world's best literature." But it is more; it is Scripture. There is a difference between the two things: Literature is the letter; Scripture is the letter inbreathed by the Holy Spirit (2 Timothy 3:16).

Other sacred books are of the earth, earthy; the Bible is the revelation from heaven—true, the mold is human, but the gold is divine. Other sacred books are man reaching after God; the Bible is the reach of God after man. Other sacred books contain man's thoughts about God; the Bible contains God's thoughts about man.

Third, the Christian should approach the Bible with a willing and obedient mind. The key to the understanding of the Scriptures lies in consecration, not scholarship; in surrender of the heart, not in genius or intellect. "If anyone wants to do His will, he shall know concerning the doctrine," Jesus said (John 7:17). Christ also said: "I thank You, Father, Lord of heaven and earth, because You have hidden these things from the wise and prudent and have revealed them to babes. Even so, Father, for so it seemed good in Your sight" (Matthew 11:25–26). Pious men with no scholarship can go through the open door of truth, while scholars with no piety remain outside, fumbling with the latch.

This is not belittling scholarship. We believe in scholarship, for we need it, and all we can get of it.

Scholarship has many advantages. Given two men equally consecrated, the one ignorant and the other learned, and it is clearly evident that the learned will get more out of the Scriptures than the ignorant. We are only putting scholarship where it belongs, in a subordinate place. We are putting first things first, giving primary and supreme place to obedient faith.

The assertion that academic training is absolutely necessary to the understanding of the Scriptures must be stoutly resisted with all one's might and main. Scholarship is a good deal, but it is not everything; nor does it accomplish the greatest things in the world. The realm of the moral and spiritual is vastly superior to that of the intellectual. Coleridge said that all the mere products of the understanding tend to death. Faith men are greater than science men. A big heart is better than a big head, and a great soul is of more importance than a great mind. Knowledge shall pass away; love will abide forever.

We should not approach the Bible then—at least not primarily—with the question, How much of this can I understand? Instead let us approach it asking, How much of it am I willing to obey? The doors of the kingdom of truth swing on the hinges of obedience. All spiritual knowledge is in order to obedience. Human teaching says, "Know first, then do." Divine teaching says, "Do first, then you will know."

The fourfold requirement for a knowledge of the Scriptures is a pure heart, a simple faith, a surrendered will, and an obedient spirit. Such prerequisites are within the reach of the simplest and most humble child of God.

Resolve to conform your life to the teachings of the Scriptures as you learn them. The declared purpose of the Bible is to make bad men good; good men better; better men the best it is possible for them to be. The Scriptures purport to make ungodly men holy, holy men holier, and saints of all who believe. It is the Book of God for the man of God—to thoroughly furnish him for all good works. To surrender the heart and life to its doctrines and precepts, this is to understand the Bible.

The study of the Bible in order to enforce its doctrines or to be able to defend its teachings, essential as such study seems to be, will not yield the best results. A study of the Bible for the purpose of obedience yields the greatest fruit. Do not find fault with the Bible because it shows you your faults, as the woman who smashed the mirror because it showed her that she had freckles. The Bible is a discoverer of faults and a revealer of virtues.

The Bible was written for the purpose of helping men and women in character building: "All Scripture is given by inspiration of God, and is profitable for doctrine, for reproof, for correction, for instruction in righteousness, that the man of God may be complete, thoroughly equipped for every good work" (2 Timothy 3:16–17). The Law of Truth, as every other law, demands conformity to its requirements if its secret and power are to be obtained.

THE INSPIRED AND AUTHORITATIVE WORD OF GOD

The Christian should regard the Bible as the inspired Word of God.
"All Scripture is given by inspiration of God" (2 Timothy 3:16).

When we speak of the Bible as being *inspired*, we mean that the sacred writings are the result of a certain influence or influences exerted by God upon their authors; that the writings are "God-breathed," as the word literally means; that "no prophecy of Scripture is of any private interpretation" (that is, it did not originate with the private impulse of any particular individual). "For prophecy never came by the will of man, but holy men of God spoke as they were moved by the Holy Spirit" (2 Peter 1:20–21). We do not have in the Scriptures the meditations of men about God, but the divinely inspired thoughts and words of God about men (see 1 Thessalonians 2:13). And there is quite a difference between these two things.

The word *inspired* indicates the strong, conscious inbreathing of God into men, qualifying them to give utterance to truth. The Scriptures are the result of the divine inbreathing, just as human speech is uttered by the breathing through man's mouth. "As they were moved" indicates that the Scriptures were not written by mere men, or at their own or any other human being's suggestion, but by holy men *when* they were moved upon, compelled—yes, driven—by the promptings of the Holy Spirit. The Holy Spirit was specially and miraculously present in and with the writers of the Scriptures. The Spirit revealed to them truths that they had not known before; the Spirit guided them alike in the recording of these truths and of the transactions which they may have copied from existing material, and of those transactions and even events of which they were eye- and ear witnesses.

Thus the authors were able to present the writings with complete accuracy and without error to the minds of others. This is our claim for the original autographs of the Scriptures—that they are the inspired, authoritative, and infallible Word of God.

The Christian should regard the Bible as the Book of final authority in matters of faith and practice.
"He taught them as one having authority" (Matthew 7:29).

The Bible is not to be looked upon as advisory or suggestive, but commandatory and imperative. It is not a volume of opinions; it is a Book of commands. It does not say, "It is suggested, recommended, or advised," but "it is written"; "it is commanded." It is not only true; it is absolute and final truth. No other book dare usurp its place, authority, or function.

The Bible alone, of all books, has the right to command my life, to say what I shall believe, to command how I shall act. The Word of God shall "judge me in the last day." Yea, it is my judge now.

The questions as to what is the ultimate and final authority in matters moral and religious is always interesting. Where is the seat of authority in matters of religion? This is always the problem of the day. Various replies are given to the question.

Reason is the seat of final authority, say some. May not the intellect with the various functions be relied upon to render sure judgments? One has only to recall the grotesque fancies that have from time to time taken hold of the finest and brainiest men and led them into the grossest delusions to satisfy oneself that the seat of authority does not lie in the reason.

Not that one should throw reason away in matters of religion: for while faith is often above reason, it is by no means contrary to it. Faith is opposed not to reason, but to sight. The voice of reason, however, is not to be considered final and authoritative. Reason is only one of the human faculties, and it, equally with others, has been affected by sin. Then there is an objective revelation outside of reason.

Can we not depend upon *conscience*, that delicate and sensitive faculty, to admonish us of evil, to praise us for the good, and settle for the right and wrong of matters religious? We have but to recall into what incalculable mischief the consciences of some men have led them—Saul of Tarsus, for example—to speedily recognize that we must look elsewhere for our authority.

There are people who claim that the church is the ultimate authority in matters of faith and practice. This is the position of the Roman Catholic Church. Called of God, divinely founded, with perpetual witness to the truth, with bishops and councils—surely the church is a sufficient guide. Yet what enormities have flourished under the banner of the church! As long as she is composed of fallible human beings, the church can never be final and authoritative in matters of faith and practice.

For our Master Himself, the Scriptures were considered sufficient authority in matters of faith and practice. It would repay anyone to look up all the passages in which these words of the Master occur: "Is it not written?" "Have you not read?" "What do the Scriptures say?" "It is written . . ." A careful study of such verses will reveal the fact that Christ referred to the Scriptures as the authority that settled matters of faith and practice for Him. Should the Bible be less to the church than it was to the church's Master? We think not.

A Roman Catholic priest on being asked to prove that the church, i.e., the Roman Catholic Church, is

the final authority referred the inquirer to Matthew
16:18–19, "You are Peter, and on this rock," etc., saying: "There is my authority for claiming authority for
my church." Do you not see the ludicrousness of his
position—he had to fall back on the Scriptures for
authority to prove that his church had any authority.
So the Bible, in the last analysis, is the final authority.

THE BIBLE AS A SPIRITUAL BOOK

*The Bible is a spiritual book—the Book of God for the man and
woman of God.*
"But the natural man does not receive the things of
the Spirit of God, . . . nor can he know them, because
they are spiritually discerned" (1 Corinthians 2:14).

There must needs be a *spiritual affinity* existing between the student of the Word of God and the Word
itself. The Holy Spirit, who taught those holy men of
old how and what to write, is the One who alone can
teach men today how to read the sacred writings. He
who inspired them must illumine now. The sundial is a
useful instrument, but of what use is it without the
sun? So it is with the Bible; its truth cannot be seen or
understood unless by the aid of the Holy Spirit. The
Bible was not written for the scientist, the geologist,
the anthropologist, or the scholar, as such; it was written for "the man of God" (2 Timothy 3:16). And that is
the reason why many a poor, illiterate "man of God"

has gone clear into the kingdom of truth while many a mere scholar has been fumbling with the latch trying to get in.

Much is said today with regard to different kinds of criticism: historical, exegetical, literary, philological. They may all be well in their proper place, but they are absolutely useless and worse than useless unless they are saturated with and controlled by that *spiritual criticism* which is so necessary to qualify and control all the rest, both natural and supernatural. This is the spirit and culture that has saved the Bible.

The scholars have never saved the Bible. They never will. They have torn it to pieces, and had it not been divine and contained within it the hiding of the life of God, the old Book would have been wrecked upon the shores of scholarly destructive criticisms years ago. Remember, all the science in the world has never smoothed a dying pillow or supplied a hope in death. The Bible has and will continue to do so.

CHAPTER TWO
❧

```
┌─────────────────────────────┐
│        THE BIBLE:           │
│       ITS AUTHORITY         │
└─────────────────────────────┘
```

OVER THE YEARS, CRITICS have objected to the Bible's reliability. They have attacked its accuracy and its authenticity as the Word of God. Let's look at both issues to determine its authority and reliability.

Frequently the Christian hears it said that "science is against the Bible" and that the Scriptures' reliability have been seriously attacked and affected by the "latest results of science." Soon, we are told, we will have two Bibles: the Bible of the scientist and scholar and the Bible of the saint.

Among some of the Bible narratives which science is declared to have injured the authority and reliability may be mentioned two: the incident of Joshua commanding the sun to stand still and the narrative of Jonah and the whale. Let us take a look at these two narratives and see if they actually are a stumbling block to unique claims of the Bible.

JOSHUA COMMANDING THE SUN TO STAND STILL

This incident in the sacred Scriptures has been cited as a scientific objection to the authority and integrity of the Word of God. It has been cited as a proof that the Bible is not a reliable revelation, for Joshua 10:12–14 speaks of the sun and moon standing still. But the sun does not move at all, scientists remind us; the earth revolves around the sun.

The Bible in describing scientific facts uses the language of appearances rather than accuracy, just as we do in this advanced, scientific age. Take up any daily newspaper in this twentieth century, and you will read, "The sun or the moon rises"; "The sun or the moon sets" at such an hour. But does it? Is not our modern newspaper guilty of a most flagrant scientific mistake, and one which our modern scientist does not seem anxious to correct? Even in this day we speak of the "dew falling," although we know that the dew does not fall, but, on the contrary, rises.

In defense of these false scientific statements we are told, "This is the way these things *appear* to us as we look at them. Although in reality it is not so, this is the accepted language of scientific *appearance*, not scientific accuracy." Why should we not be as charitable with the Bible, then? Because the Bible in describing facts of science uses the language of appearances rather than scientific accuracy, is it therefore "unscientific"? Of course not. The Bible was not written for scientists alone but for all kinds and conditions of people.

Did Joshua command the sun and moon to stand still in the midst of the heavens? It is to be regretted that many of those who attack certain narratives in the Bible are not more thoroughly acquainted with what the Bible actually says and especially with the original languages in which these events were written. The knowledge of four Hebrew words used in Joshua's story would help much in the understanding of that miracle. Because of such ignorance, writers have given different positions of the sun at the time of Joshua's command. One so-called scholar writes, "If the expression 'above Gibeon' be exact, then the early morning must be intended; if 'in the midst of the heaven,' then it must be the noonday." It does not seem to have occurred to this writer in what a laughable position he thus places himself in that he is thereby picturing Joshua as commanding the sun not to go down *early in the morning,* or at its height at *noon.*

The word translated "stand still" in Joshua 10:12 means to be *dumb,* or *silent,* to *wait,* to *rest,* to *tarry.* Thirty times in the Old Testament it is so rendered; and in no other place, save here, is it translated "stand still." The word, therefore, should be translated "tarry" or "wait."

The words "in the midst of" in verse 13 mean literally "the half of," and not the "midst" or the "middle." In more than 106 cases it is so translated (cf. "half of their beards," 2 Samuel 10:4. They could not shave off one middle, but one half).

Thus verse 13 should read, "So the sun rested, waited, or tarried in the *half* of the heavens." By the "half of the heavens" is meant, of course, the visible horizon—at least so the ancients, who were acquainted with the whole circle of the earth, understood it. The command of Joshua, therefore, was for the sun, which was about to go down into the invisible half of the heaven, to remain in sight.

We are told that the "sun stood still in the midst [half] of the heaven, and did not hasten to go down." The words "did not hasten " do not mean to stand still absolutely. When we say that a man does not hasten, we do not necessarily mean that he stands still. Literally, verses 12–14 may read: "There Joshua is speaking to Jehovah, and says before the eyes of Israel, 'Sun over Gibeon, tarry; and moon in the valley of Aijalon', and the sun is tarrying, and the moon stays, till the nation is avenged of their enemies. Is not this written in the book of the upright, and the sun is tarrying in the half of the heavens, and it does not hasten to set as (or for) a complete day; and there has not been any like this day before it or after it."

One has well said: "If the sun were near setting, the rays would fall on Gibeon on the east, and it would continue in sight, as it does at the pole of the earth for weeks together; and there was no day like it, when, his light shining the night through, two consecutive days formed one day. The miracle remains; it was the work of almighty God. A slight dip of the pole, or deflection of the rays of light, or ways unknown to men, might have accomplished this remarkable miracle."

Was there any sufficient reason why God should thus miraculously interpose in behalf of Israel? We think so. Israel, for probably the first time, was confronted by the combined forces of the Ammonites and the Gibeonites, the objects of whose worship were the sun and moon. In a sense, the battle was a battle between the gods of those nations and Jehovah, the God of Israel. This being the case, we can see why it should be shown on that day who was the true God. The gods of the Ammonites and Gibeonites were powerless before the God of Israel and, indeed, were compelled to favor God's chosen people and minister to the destruction of their own deluded worshipers. The plagues of Egypt were a battle between the gods of Egypt and Jehovah, the God of Israel. Why not this battle, then?

JONAH AND THE BIG FISH

Objections to the reliability of the Bible revelation have been made on the ground of the unreasonableness of the story of Jonah and the whale. It is contended by some that the record of this event is not reliable because it is impossible for a whale to swallow a man, not having a gullet large enough. Further, it is contended that no man could live in the belly of a whale for so long a time.

Since the publication of Bullen's *Cruise of the Cachalot,* in which the author describes his whaling expeditions and declares facts concerning these sea monsters that harmonize perfectly with the Bible story, skeptics have been compelled to swallow their objections.

The critics of the story of Jonah based their arguments for the impossibility of a whale swallowing a man on their knowledge of the structure of a Greenland whale only, whereas we now know that there are over sixty kinds of whales. Dr. Thomas Beale, a surgeon of London, in his work entitled *Observations on the Natural History of the Spermecete Whale* (page 294), in describing a sea monster of this kind says: "The throat is capacious enough to give passage to the body of a man, presenting a strong contrast to the contracted gullet of the Greenland whale."

It ought to be noted in this connection that the Book of Jonah does not say that it was "a whale," but "a great fish," or, as the Revised Version of Matthew translates it, "a sea monster" that swallowed the prophet. Surely if God could create a sea monster at all, He could create one, even a whale, with a mouth and gullet large enough to swallow a man. A skeptic was once arguing against the story of Baalam's ass speaking. His friend said, "Well, if you will make an ass, I will make him talk." Ability to create carries with it the power to endow with such powers as the Creator wishes.

It is remarkable to note that the great fish was "prepared" to swallow Jonah. This word *prepared* occurs four times in Jonah, and only in three other places in the whole Bible, although the ordinary word *prepared* occurs hundreds of times. This word indicates that God *appointed in a special way* this fish to swallow Jonah, just as in the New Testament Jesus appointed a special fish to have a coin in its mouth at the appointed time and place (Matthew 17:27).

In the book of Jonah, God "appointed" or "prepared" four special things: "a great fish to swallow Jonah" (1:17); "a plant and made it come up over Jonah" (4:6); "a vehement east wind" (4:8); "a worm" to smite the plant (4:7). These four words indicated a miraculous manifestation of God's power for a specific purpose. As Anderson noted, "That the Almighty could, if necessary, extemporize a sea monster for the assigned purpose we should not doubt. To say that God *could not* do this is to deny God altogether; to say He *would not* do it is absurd—any one of us would do it in similar circumstances if only he had the power."

JONAH: A TYPE OF CHRIST

By this extraordinary occurrence—a prophet removed by a great fish and then returned to earth three days later—Jonah became one of the most remarkable types of the death, burial, and resurrection of the Lord

Jesus to be found anywhere in the Old Testament Scriptures: "For as Jonah was three days and three nights in the belly of a great fish, so will the Son of Man be three days and three nights in the heart of the earth" (Matthew 12:40). And the one is as much a fact as the other.

The New Testament refers to Jonah as a prophecy of the resurrection of Christ; for He rose again the third day *according to Scriptures;* and where, except in Jonah, shall we find in the Old Testament a plain and clear prophecy of His rising on the third day? It was to the "sign of the prophet Jonah" that Jesus referred. It cannot be that the great fact of all history—namely, the resurrection of Jesus Christ—is based upon a myth.

The reality of the events of the book of Jonah are attested by the words of Jesus: "The men of Nineveh will rise in the judgment with this generation and condemn it, because they repented at the preaching of Jonah; and indeed a greater than Jonah is here" (Matthew 12:41). It surely would have been absurd for Jesus to have compared Himself to or contrasted Himself with a myth by saying, "and indeed a greater than a myth is here." That Jonah was a real person is clearly stated in 2 Kings 14:25: "The Lord God of Israel . . . had spoken through His servant Jonah the son of Amittai, the prophet who was from Gath Hepher." A myth has no father or birthplace, nor does it speak.

We should remember that the preservation of Jonah alive for so long a time in the sea monster was a miraculous event, just as the resurrection of Jesus Christ, of which the story of Jonah was a type, was a miraculous display of God's power; and for this reason it was a sign to the Ninevites.

There are those who are inclined to think that Jonah really died and was raised again from the dead, and thus was "brought up . . . from the pit [corruption]," (cf. Jonah 2:2, 6) just as Jesus died and was raised again, and saw no corruption. Such persons maintain that in this case Jonah was more accurately a type of Christ's *death, burial,* and *resurrection*. Even if such an interpretation would be valid, the supernatural element in the story would still remain, for whether Jonah was preserved alive, or died and was raised from the dead, both actions call for a miraculous display of divine power.

JESUS' BELIEF IN THE RELIABILITY OF THE BIBLE

The approach of the Christian to the Bible must be like the approach of the Christian's Master, the Lord Jesus Christ. It surely should go without controversy that what was sufficient for the Master ought to be sufficient for the church. What was the attitude of Christ towards the Scriptures? How did the Savior regard the Word of God? If we can settle these questions, we have settled the attitude of the Christian towards it.

First of all, it is clear from the words of Jesus that *Christ accepted the narratives and events He referred to as being*

historical and true. He referred to the story of Creation, the Garden of Eden, Adam and Eve (cf. Matthew 19:3–6 with Genesis 2:24); the Flood, Sodom and Gomorrah, Lot and Lot's wife (Luke 17:26–33), for example, as being occurrences of actual history. These were not myths or allegories to the great Teacher sent from God, to Him who was and is "the wisdom of God."

Critics may say that Jesus accepted the current views of His time regarding these things, which is virtually saying that He did not know any better. If so, then what becomes of His being the Truth, or of being omniscient and knowing all things? If He did not know these things, how can we depend on His Word with reference to deeper things, those things that pertain to the spiritual and eternal interests? Surely no *kenotic* theory of self-emptying must be held that robs Christ of His place as the infallible Teacher. Jesus put the stamp of His approval on these things—and, strange to say, they are the very things which destructive criticism says are myths—as being historical and true. If these things were sufficient for the Master, are they not sufficient for the church? We think so.

In the second place, *Jesus Christ accepted the Scriptures as the inspired and authoritative Word of God.* He claimed that David could "in [or by] the Spirit call Him [the Son of David] Lord" (Matthew 22:43). He called the Scriptures "the Word of God" as contrasted with the traditions of men: "Making the word of God of no effect through your tradition" (Mark 7:13).

In matters of doctrine, Jesus appealed to the Bible as being final and authoritative. When the question of divorce and its grounds came up for settlement (Mark 10:2–12), was it not to the Word of God as found in Genesis 2 that Jesus referred them for the solution of the problem? When the Sadducees, who did not believe in a resurrection, tried to trap Him by putting hard questions regarding the future life (Luke 20:27–40), did He not again refer them to what was said to Moses at the bush (Exodus 3:6) as a direct and authoritative answer to their skepticism? When the Pharisees wondered about His deity (Matthew 22:42–45), to what did He refer them for a conclusive answer? Was it not to the Psalms (110:1)?

In matters of duty, Jesus used "the sword of the Spirit, which is the word of God" to ward off the attacks of Satan in the wilderness. Three times in the wilderness temptation, Jesus replied, "It is written." These are Christ's answers; not eloquent and original, but quotations from the Bible that anyone can use. Can we do better in meeting the temptations of life? We see here, surely, Christ's own estimate of the Scriptures.

Again and again, when religious leaders appealed to Christ to settle some debatable question of conduct, He replied, "What do the Scriptures say?" "Have you not read?" "Go and read what that means." Frequently, He appealed to the Scriptures as the ultimate authority in matters of faith and practice. "You are mistaken, not knowing the Scriptures."

It is exceedingly important for us to understand this phase of the subject in this day when so much is made of the *inner light* as compared with the *objective revelation*—the sacred Scriptures. Surely Jesus had the "inner light" more than we all, did He not? Yet, when it comes to matters of faith and practice, He referred to an objective revelation—the Word of God as the final authority.

The attitude of the Redeemer is worthy of imitation by the redeemed.

ACCURATE TRANSMISSION OF THE ORIGINAL TEXT

The Bible, as we have it today, can be traced back to its original sources. To substantiate this claim, let us follow three lines of proof.

First, there is the proof from printed copies of the Bible. Printed copies of the Scriptures are extant today, dating as far back as the middle of the fifteenth century. In the library of Exeter College, Oxford, there is a copy of the Old Testament in Hebrew, dated A.D. 1488. In the Royal Library, Berlin, there is a Hebrew copy of the Old Testament, dated A.D. 1494. It was from this copy that Luther made his German translation of the Scriptures. There are extant printed copies of the New Testament in Greek, dated A.D. 1516, and edited by Erasmus; in Latin, dated A.D. 1514.

These printed copies, on being compared, agree in the main with the printed copies of the Bible we possess in this year of our Lord 1922. Thus we prove, by a single step, that the Old and the New Testaments, in the form we have them now, existed four hundred years ago. This evidence is open to the investigation of both Christian and skeptic.

But if the printed copies of the Bible take us back to the middle of the fifteenth century, the question may be asked, "What are you going to do about all the centuries between the fifteenth and the days of the apostles?" This question, difficult as it may seem, is not impossible to answer. There are manuscripts of the Scriptures which take us back to the middle of the fourth century. Thus our second proof: *the proof of the manuscripts.*

At the time of the first printed copy of the Bible, Christian scholars possessed no less than two thousand such manuscripts, certainly a sufficient number to establish the integrity of the sacred text. If scholars are willing to accept ten or twenty copies at most of any classical writer as proving the genuineness and authenticity of his writings (which is certainly true), how much more ought we to be willing to admit the same for the Scriptures, with over two thousand manuscripts! All these manuscripts, when compared, agree with the printed copies of the Scriptures which we possess today.

The question may be asked, "Why do these manuscripts date back as far only as the fourth century?" The answer may be found in the historic fact that in the year A.D. 302 Emperor Diocletian ordered the wholesale destruction of the sacred books. Again, it should be remembered that in the year A.D. 330 the Emperor Constantine ordered a large number of copies of the sacred Scriptures to be made for use in the churches of his day. This accounts for the large number of manuscripts dating from the fourth century.

The manuscripts we are here speaking of contain, separately, only parts of the Scriptures. When put together and compared, however, they contain the whole Bible. Indeed, some of them contain the New Testament in full. Thus we see that, as far back as the middle of the fourth century, the same Bible as that which we have now was in existence. The Bible of the fourth and the twentieth centuries are one and the same.

We are still, however, especially so far as the New Testament is concerned, about three or four hundred years removed from the lifetime of the writers of the New Testament. How can we bridge this gulf? The answer is found in the third proof: *the proof from church and apostolic fathers.*

From the time of the death of the apostle John, about A.D. 100, until about the fourth century, there arose in the Christian church certain defenders of the truth of the Christian religion, called *apologists.* These men are known as "the church fathers." In their religious controversies with the enemies of Christianity, as well as in their letters of instruction to Christians and churches, they made constant use of Scripture quotations.

These are called the "Quotations of the Church Fathers." These quotations were made with great exactness. Indeed many of them are given verbatim. So numerous are these quotations, we are told, that were the New Testament blotted out of existence it could be restored entire, excepting eleven verses.

Between the church fathers and the apostles themselves, however, another gap occurs, which is filled in by the apostolic fathers; i. e., by men who were alive before the last of the apostles passed away. Polycarp (A.D. 69–155), a disciple of the apostle John, and Clement of Rome, who was doubtless a companion of Paul (Philippians 4:3), were among the apostolic fathers. References are made to every part of the New Testament in the writings of these men. The New Testament must therefore have been in existence at the time of their writing.

Thus, step-by-step we are able to prove that the Bible (the New Testament at least—the Old we shall consider later) as we have it today is the same as that which existed in the days of the apostles. Our faith in God's Word rests upon no cunningly devised fables; it rests upon evidence, and any earnest, seeking soul can gain access to such evidence if he so desires. An earnest, intelligent search in the public reference libraries of any of our large cities will corroborate the truth here set forth.

PROOFS FOR THE AUTHENTICITY OF THE OLD TESTAMENT MANUSCRIPTS

No doubt should now be left in our minds regarding the genuineness of the New Testament. But how about the Old Testament? Is the evidence for its genuineness and authenticity as abundant and convincing? Let's see the proofs for the authenticity and authority of the Old Testament.

First, there is the testimony of Christ. Christ had the Old Testament in His possession. No one can read the Gospels carefully without being impressed with Christ's marvelous knowledge of the Old Testament. Not only in His defense during the wilderness temptation but throughout His entire career, the Master showed a remarkable familiarity with the Hebrew Scriptures.

Were these Scriptures the same as we have them today?

That Christ constantly refers to the Sacred Writings, there can be no doubt. If one should go through the Gospels and mark every reference made by Christ to the Old Testament, it would be found that a very large number of the Old Testament books were referred to and quoted by Him. Now, this being true, it is self-evident that the books quoted from were in existence in our Lord's day.

Further, it is to be noted that our Lord not only quoted largely and freely from the Old Testament

Scriptures, but that He referred to the sacred volume, as a whole, as possessing the same divisions into which we divide it today: the Law, the Prophets, and the Psalms. "Then He said to them, 'These are the words which I spoke to you while I was still with you, that all things must be fulfilled which were written in the Law of Moses and the Prophets and the Psalms concerning Me'" (Luke 24:44).

There is no just reason to doubt that the Old Testament, as we have it today, was in existence in our Lord's day.

Second, there is the testimony of the apostles. The apostles and writers of the New Testament possessed the Old Testament as we have it today. When Paul speaks of the "Scriptures" that Timothy had known from his childhood, he refers to the Old Testament. Peter's reference to the Scriptures coming "not in old time by the will of man (2 Peter 1:21 KJV)," and John's allusion to the Scriptures being "fulfilled," all point to the Old Testament.

The quotations from and allusions to the Old Testament in the New are of a surprisingly large number. The direct quotations amount to 263. The allusions or references that are less direct number 376, making a total of 639. There are ninety quotations from the Pentateuch, and references to them which amount to over one hundred. The Psalms are directly quoted from seventy-one times, references and allusions being made to them upwards of thirty times. The prophecy of Isaiah is directly quoted from fifty-six times and referred and alluded to forty-eight times. The Minor Prophets are quoted from and referred to about thirty times.

Third, there is the testimony of the Septuagint. From the above mentioned testimony, it is obvious that there existed in the days of the apostles and Christ the Old Testament as we have it today. Indeed, it can be clearly proven that the Old Testament existed even before our Lord's day. An edition of the Hebrew Scriptures translated into the Greek language and called the Septuagint Version was in existence two hundred and eighty-five years before our Lord's birth. According to tradition, this version was translated from the Hebrew by seventy-two Jews, each of whom, in a separate cell, made a complete translation of the entire Old Testament. This translation was made in Alexandria about the time of Ptolemy Philadelphus (285 B.C.). There is no need at this time for a discussion of the manner in which this translation of the Hebrew Scriptures was made. It is sufficient for the present purpose to know that as far back as the year 285 B.C. there was a copy of the Old Testament Scriptures, copies of which exist today, and which, on being compared, agree as to the matter, form, and structure with the last copy of the Old Testament that leaves the press this year.

THE VERY WORD OF GOD

From the evidence we have submitted, it can be

said that the entire Bible as we have it today is indeed and in truth the very Word of God, written by the men whose names it bears, and with the text essentially unchanged, as genuine and authentic, as it was when it left the hands of the sacred writers. As the hymn writer correctly noted:

How firm a foundation, ye saints of the Lord,
Is laid for your faith in His excellent Word!

"Heaven and earth will pass away, but My words will by no means pass away," Jesus said (Mark 13:31). In this day of crumbling creeds and confessions; in this day when men are not satisfied with the simple sound of the gospel trumpet, but seek a gospel with variations; in this day when the exclamation mark of faith is being displaced by the interrogation mark of doubt and unbelief, it is a grand and glorious thing for the Christian to know that the Word of God stands sure. As the psalmist wrote, "Forever, O Lord, Your word is settled in heaven" (Psalm 119:89).

CHAPTER THREE

GOD

TO MANY CHRISTIANS, GOD is what He was to the Athenians: an "unknown God," a being who is "ignorantly" worshiped (Acts 17:23 KJV). We do not know God as we may or should. It is certainly possible for us and obligatory upon us to know Him better than we do. The more intelligently we know God, the better pleasing and effective our service for Him may be. The more we know God, the greater the evidence of His power and presence in our lives.

Of course, no man can know God perfectly. A God capable of human comprehension would not be God. A perfect knowledge of God is not, however, necessary to be well-pleasing to Him, and to enjoy His favor and blessing. Millions of people are using and receiving untold blessings from the telephone, telegraph, and electricity who know scarcely more about these marvels of inventive genius than to take down the ear trumpet, speak into the mouthpiece, turn the switch, press the button, or write the message. It surely is not necessary for a man to understand all the intricate mechanism of his watch in order that he may know the time. If he has sense enough to wind it up, that is sufficient. So it is with regard to our knowledge of God. Perfect knowledge is not necessary to enjoy His presence and favor and to render to Him intelligent service.

Yet there is a certain knowledge of God which is necessary in order to be saved (see, for instance, John 17:3; Romans 10:17), and for the continued exercise of trust and confidence in the divine dealings. "They that know thy name will put their trust in thee." "Then shall we know, if we follow on to know the Lord" (Psalm 9:10; Hosea 6:3 KJV). We should endeavor to know as much of God as He has been pleased to reveal of Himself and purposes in nature, history, providence, and, foremost and above all, in the Bible. In that way we may apprehend, to some fair degree and commensurate with our highest relation to Him, who and what He is, and what are His purposes for mankind and the world. Following are some of the facts every intelligent Christian should know concerning God.

THE EXISTENCE OF GOD

The Scriptures do not attempt to *prove* the existence of God. It is a fact everywhere taken for granted (Genesis 1:1). It is assumed, too, that all men everywhere have a certain kind of knowledge of God. This knowledge is intuitive, acquired, or both. No tribe of men has as yet been discovered, no matter how low in the scale of civilization such human beings may be, that are without some knowledge of God, however crude or grotesque. Surely God has "put eternity in their hearts" (Ecclesiastes 3:11).

Hume, the skeptic, said one day to his friend Ferguson, "Adam, there is a God." Voltaire, the atheist, prayed to God in a thunderstorm. Even Robert G. Ingersoll, the once famous infidel, disclaimed being an atheist. He said, "I am not an atheist for I do not say there is no God; I am an agnostic—I do not know." A professed atheist, addressing a coterie of his followers, said, "I have gotten rid of the idea of a supreme being, and *I thank God for it.*" But had he?

No one can dismiss the idea. The knowledge of God is born with every person, male and female. Only God Himself could have planted in the human heart such a universal belief—and the very universality of the belief vouches for its truth.

As the writer of Hebrews noted, "He who comes to God must believe that He is" (11:6).

Reason tells us God exists.
"For since the creation of the world His invisible attributes are clearly seen, being understood by the things that are made, even His eternal power and Godhead, so that they are without excuse" (Romans 1:20).

Of course, there are arguments and evidences proving (or probably setting forth) the existence of God outside of the declarations of the Bible. There is the deduction which every honest, thinking man must make from a consideration of the universe, creation, nature, man, and all living creatures. *Reason* compels a man to believe that these things did not come into being of themselves. No adequate cause outside of God can account for such wondrous and superhuman effects.

As the apostle Paul noted in Romans 1:20, who, that observes the providence around about him every day, can come to any other reasonable and satisfactory conclusion than that "there's a divinity that shapes our ends," and that there is sufficient evidence that the happenings of life are of divine permission, will, control, and intelligence?

Our conscience tells us God exists.
"Who show the work of the law written in their hearts, their conscience also bearing witness, and between themselves their thoughts accusing or else excusing them" (Romans 2:15).

Conscience is an evidence of the existence of God. There is a something in man that says, "I ought" or "I ought not" to act thus under given circumstances. There is a tribunal within man that passes judgment upon all his acts, and says, "This is right," or "This is wrong"; a something that excuses or accuses, approves or condemns. Cardinal Newman said it was this "voice of God in the heart and conscience that keep him from being an atheist," that compelled belief in God.

Every man knows that he is responsible to *God* and not to man for some things, and that there is a higher than human tribunal before which he stands and is daily, hourly, judged. That I am responsible to a moral Governor far higher than man must be true. I am certain of it; I feel it within me. It cannot but be true. Conscience compels me to believe it. Such being the case, there must be such a divine, moral being who has the right to control, command, condemn, and commend, and to whom I must some day give account.

Our experiences and observation tell us God exists.
"O Lord, I know the way of man is not in himself; it is not in man who walks to direct his own steps" (Jeremiah 10:23).

The *experiences* of man teach him that there is a God. There are events, calamities, deliverances, interferences, and provisions and withholdings in human experience that cannot fairly or legitimately be traced to any other source than that of a controlling, superintending Power that is not limited and human, but divine and supreme. Solomon wrote, "A man's steps are of the Lord. . . . A man's heart plans his way, but the Lord directs his steps" (Proverbs 20:24; 16:9).

Intelligent *observation* of nature and life, setting forth as they do the great fact of intelligent design and purpose in all things, should lead the thoughtful and reverent observer and student inevitably to faith in a personal God, a supreme, divine Intelligence. Patton said, "Belief in a personal self-existent God is in harmony with all the facts of our mental and moral nature. . . . Atheism leaves all these matters without an explanation, and makes, not history alone, but our intellectual and moral nature itself, an [impostor] and a lie." Belief in God is a key that fits all the wards of the lock of life; therefore we know that we have the right key.

No one but a "fool" (Psalm 14:1; Romans 1:22), the grossly immoral or the intellectually biased (Romans 1:18–32), will deny the existence of a personal, intelligent, moral, and supreme Being—God. As someone has well said: "What! No God? A watch, and no key for it? A watch with a mainspring broken, and no jeweler to fix it? A watch, and no repair shop? A time-card and a train, and nobody to run it? A star lit, and nobody to pour oil in to keep the wick burning? Flowers, and no florist? Conditions, and no conditioner?" He who sits in the heavens shall laugh at such absurd atheism.

THE NATURE AND BEING OF GOD

God is Spirit.

"'God is Spirit'" (John 4:24).

"'A spirit does not have flesh and bones'" (Luke 24:39).

The idea that God has a body with parts and passions like a man is excluded by the above words of Jesus. The scriptural statement that man was made "in the image of God" (Genesis 1:26) does not refer to physical but to moral and spiritual qualities and likeness (Ephesians 4:24; Colossians 3:10).

God cannot be located in any one place on the earth to the exclusions of another. The mistake the Jew, Samaritan, and Greek made were to suppose that God could thus be located (John 4:19–21; Acts 7:47–49; 17:24, 29).

No one knows how God looks, nor can human imagination conceive of His appearance. For this reason the Israelites were forbidden to make idols resembling God (Deuteronomy 4:15–18; Isaiah 40:25). "No one has seen God at any time" (John 1:18), nor has any "seen His form" (John 5:37). Men like Moses and the seventy elders have seen manifestations of God, but no one has ever seen God as He really is, in His true essence (Exodus 24:10; 33:18–23). Manifestations of God in visible form are recorded in the Bible in the Old Testament (including to Abraham in Genesis 16:7, 10, 13; 18:1–10; 22:11). And in the New Testament,

God revealed Himself in Christ (Colossians 1:15; Hebrews 1:3).

God is *the* Spirit, "the Father of [our] spirits" (Hebrews 12:9; Acts 17:28), the self-existent "I am" (Exodus 3:14), and the source of all life (John 5:26).

God is a Person.
"The Lord is the true God; He is the living God and the everlasting King" (Jeremiah 10:10).

The fact that God is a Person closely follows that of His being Spirit. It is erroneous to picture, describe, or think of God as an impersonal force or principle. It is equally erroneous to identify God with truth, goodness, mind, as though he were such at the expense of having any existence separate from these abstract qualities. Such a pantheistic ideal lies at the root of the fundamental error of Christian Science respecting the doctrine of the personality of God. In Eddyism, "God is Principle, not Person."

It is the clear teaching of the Scriptures of both the Old and New Testaments that God is a Person clearly distinct from nature and man. God is differentiated from idols and is called the "living" God in contradistinction to images. God is One who sees, feels, hears, sympathizes, hates, and loves. He may be angered, grieved, or sinned against. He is the Creator of all things animate and inanimate (Jeremiah 10:3–16; Acts 14:15; 1 Thessalonians 1:9). He is active and personal in the welfare of His creatures (see, for instance, Genesis 6:6; 1 Kings 11:9; Deuteronomy 6:15; Proverbs 6:16).

Personality, as used in this connection, does not necessarily include substance as we understand the word. It does, however, stand for intelligence, will, self-consciousness, self-determination, reason, mind, and individuality. All these attributes of personality God possesses and is the source of them in His creatures.

How cold, formal, uninviting is the impersonal abstraction that pantheistic religions like Christian Science would put up before us, label God, and call upon us to worship! What inducement is there to pray to so impersonal a being? Why take down the telephone to talk if you know that there is no one at the other end of the line to listen? How full of comfort is the thought of prayer and fellowship with God if, according to the Christian concept, God is a Person: loving, kind, thoughtful, actively interested in His people, listening to catch the faintest breath of prayer. We are assured that "He is, and that He is a rewarder of those who diligently seek him" (Hebrews 11:6).

Speak to Him, O soul of mine,
For He listens, and spirit with Spirit can meet.
Nearer is He than breathing,
And closer than hands and feet.

Such a God is our God.

THE ATTRIBUTES OF GOD

God has all power; He is omnipotent.
"'I know that You can do everything'" (Job 42:2).
"'With God all things are possible'" (Matthew 19:26).

Nothing is beyond the reach of the power of God. "Is anything too hard for the Lord?" (Genesis 18:14). Of course not.

In addition, all created things are the work of His great might (Genesis 1:1). The storm and the calm of the sea are of His working (Psalm 107:25–29). Earthquake, hurricane, and fire are obedient to His word and will (Nahum 1:5–6). Everything in heaven—angels, principalities, and powers—are subject to His direction and under His absolute control (Daniel 4:35; Hebrews 1:14). Even the activities of Satan are limited by the dictates of His wise and holy will (Job 1:12; 2:6; Luke 22:31–32; Revelation 20:2). The ways and actions of mankind are not beyond the power of God to control, as the experience of Pharaoh (Exodus 14), Nebuchadnezzar (Daniel 4), Saul of Tarsus (Acts 9) and mankind as a whole (James 4:13–15) clearly show.

We should not wonder, then, that men who have caught the vision of God as the almighty, wonder-working, all-powerful God have been able to do exploits for Him. Such believers as Moses before Pharaoh, Joshua before Jericho, Elijah before Ahab, and the illustrious saints portrayed in that wonderful roll of honor in Hebrews 11 triumphed with the help of God's mighty power.

Why then should we be weak when with us is prayer, and with God is power—power equal to that which raised Jesus Christ from the tomb in Joseph's garden (Ephesians 1:19–22)? If such a God be for us, as He is, who then can be against us? "'Who are you, O great mountain? Before Zerrubabel you shall become a plain!'" And all this comes "'not by might nor by power, but by My Spirit,' says the Lord of hosts" (Zecharaiah 4:6–7). If we exercise faith in so mighty a God (Mark 11:23), then nothing (that is according to His declared will and which we are called upon in the divine Word to do) will be impossible to accomplish.

Plan big things, mighty ventures for God. Attempt the humanly possible for Him. God loves to have His people put His power to the test (see, for instance, Malachi 3:10; 2 Kings 3:13–20). All power in heaven and in earth belongs to God—go therefore and do mighty things for Him.

God knows all things; He is omniscient.
"Oh, the depth of the riches both of the wisdom and knowledge of God! How unsearchable are His judgments and His ways past finding out!" (Romans 11:33).

Nothing, open or secret, is hidden from God (see Hebrews 4:13). "The eyes of the Lord are in every place, keeping watch on the evil and the good" (Proverbs 15:3). All "the ways of a man are before the eyes of the Lord, and He ponders all his paths" (5:21). No plan or purpose is hidden from God, who "declares to man what his thought is" (Amos 4:13). In Jeremiah 32:19, Jeremiah echoed Amos's words: "Your eyes are open to all the ways of the sons of men, to give everyone according to his ways and according to the fruit of his doings." How otherwise could God reward the righteous and punish the wicked?

How detailed is God's knowledge of nature! The names and number of the stars are known to Him (Psalm 147:4). What a majestic portrayal of God's knowledge of the things of nature we have in Job, chapters 38–42, especially 38:3–4, 12, 19, 33, 37.

In history nothing occurs of which God is not already aware. In Daniel, chapters 2, 4, and 8, in a striking way we have depicted the history of nations for centuries to come. "Known to God from eternity are all His works" (Acts 15:18).

God is never surprised at what happens. There is no past and future with Him. All time is one eternal present. We see but a day at a time. God sees the end from the beginning and all that lies between (Isaiah 46:9–10; Acts 15:18). On a desk lie two calendars: one is composed of 365 days and displays but one day at a time; the other consists of but one sheet, but thereon may be found the exact day of the week, for example, on which any day occurred for 100 years backwards or forwards. Our calendar is a daily, yea, hourly one; God's calendar is eternal.

Not one thing occurs in the history of mankind as a whole or pertaining to any single individual but what God knows. He knew the afflictions through which His chosen people were passing (Exodus 3:7). He well knew what stand Pharaoh would take (3:19). What intimate knowledge of individual action is portrayed in Psalm 139! He knows it all.

How heart searching, and yet how comforting, too, is the thought of the omniscience of God. How careful we should be as to the nature of the thoughts, plans, and purposes we allow to lodge in our minds and hearts. How careful regarding the things done in secret, the things we may be tempted to do in the dark and in the chambers of our imagery (Ezekiel 8:12) when we are prone to think we are unobserved.

What comfort to know that God is willing to bestow this "wisdom which is from above" upon His creatures (James 1:5; 1 Kings 3:9–12). How sweet to read the "I know" so oft repeated in the letters to the seven churches in Revelation (2:2, 9, 13, 19; 3:1, 8, 15), even though sometimes it be the "I know" of rebuke. To be assured that God knows our trials, suffering, temptations, and patience under great stress, as well as our victories and good and brave deeds, is indeed a great encouragement. Too often our friends see only our failure; they do not know how hard we tried to win. God knows! God sees! God cares!

God is omnipresent; He is everywhere.
"Where can I go from Your Spirit? Or where can I flee from Your presence?" (Psalm 139:7).
"'Can any hide himself in secret places, so I shall not see him?' says the Lord" (Jeremiah 23:24).

There is no place in heaven, sky, earth, sea, yea, even hell, where it can be said, "God is not." "The eyes of the Lord are in every place, keeping watch on the evil and the good," wrote Solomon (Proverbs 15:3). God can see idols even in the heart or that are worshiped under ground (Ezekiel 14:7; 8:5–18), as well as the sin which is plain to every eye.

Yet, while God is everywhere present, He is not thus present in the same sense. Such a belief would be pantheistic and, of course, erroneous. God is in heaven, for example, in a special sense, in a sense that He is not elsewhere: Heaven is His "dwelling place" (Matthew 6:9; 7:11). Yet God is everywhere—everywhere actively interested in the welfare of His people and in carrying out His redemptive purposes.

Does God see what a man does in secret? Is the divine eye an eternal detective? Then how careful should we be in all manner of living! When tempted to sin in secret, we should remember that God sees all and respond, "How can I sin, and do 'this evil in Your sight'?" (Psalm 51:4).

Yet, notwithstanding, what a blessing to know that God is always near; that He is not so far off as even to be nigh. What a blessing to know that He is within, closer than breathing, and nearer than hands or feet. The hymn writer correctly noted:

I know not where His islands lift their fronded palms in the air;
I only know I cannot drift beyond His love and care.

God is eternal.
"I am who I am" (Exodus 3:14).

God is without beginning or end. There never was a time when God was not; there will never be a time when He will cease to be. He is the eternal "I am"— the eternal past, present, and future of all existence, the everlasting God. Scriptures that proclaim His eternality include Deuteronomy 33:27; Psalm 90:2; and Isaiah 40:28; 57:15.

What a comfort for believers to know that we are "partakers of the divine nature" (2 Peter 1:4); that the life of God is our life (John 5:24–29); that we abide even as God abides (1 John 2:17).

God is immutable; He is unchangeable.
"For I am the Lord, I do not change " (Malachi 3:6).

God is unchangeable in His nature (1 Samuel 15:29; James 1:17). The divine mind never changes. God does not think about one thing in a certain manner one day, and the next day in a different manner. True, we are told in the Scriptures that God "repents" (Genesis 6:6; Jonah 3:10 KJV), but by such an expression we are to understand not a change in the divine purpose, but a change in the divine *dealings* with mankind insofar as man changes from sin to righteousness or vice versa. Divine repentance, therefore, is the same principle in the divine character acting differently under altered circumstances. The divine *mind* and *character* never change. They are always the same in their attitude towards the righteous and the sinner.

God's dealings with men do change from time to time, even as people change in their conduct. Such must inevitably be the case, seeing God is absolutely holy and righteous. "When a man, bicycling against the wind, turns about and goes with the wind instead of going against it, the wind seems to change, although it is blowing just as it was before."

How grand it is to feel that there is One who never fails, changes, or disappoints us! His word and promise may be absolutely depended upon. "Has He said, and will He not do? Or has He spoken, and will He not make it good?" (Numbers 23:19). My soul, have you cast your all upon the word and promise of God for forgiveness, pardon, peace, eternal life? Then you shall not be disappointed. "Heaven and earth may pass away"; but not one word of God shall fail. All shall come to pass.

God is holy.
"Holy, holy, holy, is the Lord of hosts" (Isaiah 6:3).
"God is light and in Him is no darkness at all" (1 John 1:5).

If any distinction at all can be made between the attributes of God—whether omnipotence, omnipresence, omniscience, etc.—the divine holiness is the one attribute which God would have His people think of as standing out above all the others. Such was the revelation of God received by Moses (Exodus 34:6–9), Job (Job 40:1–12), and Isaiah (6:1–8). About thirty times in the prophecy of Isaiah God is called "the Holy One." As in a photograph in which we desire to see not the hands or feet but the face, so in God we should desire to see the divine holiness more than the divine power and knowledge. Only that way shall we be able to see sin in its blackness and awfulness, the need and necessity of atonement, and the wondrous grace of God in providing a way of life for sinful men.

When we speak of the holiness of God, we mean the consummate and perfect purity and the sanctity of the divine nature; that God is free from all iniquity both in Himself and in His dealings with men. God is "of purer eyes than to behold evil, and cannot look on wickedness" (Habakkuk 1:13).

The divine holiness manifests itself in God's actions and dealings. God cannot do wrong, nor can He act unjustly. However much Job may have thought that he was being unfairly dealt with, such a conclusion was nevertheless false. "Far be it from God to do wickedness, and from the Almighty to commit iniquity" (Job 34:10). However hidden and mysterious God's dealings with us may be, they are always right and just. Being holy, God must, of course, punish sin and reward righteousness. He is the uncompromising foe of sin. So much does God hate sin and desire to deliver His people from its guilt, tyranny, and power that He has given His only begotten Son to redeem us from all iniquity.

In like manner God loves and rewards the righteous, for He loves holiness in His creatures (Hebrews 1:9), and has sacrificed greatly to bring about such qualities in them.

The doctrine of the divine holiness makes certain demands upon us. Every child of God should make it his constant aim to be holy even as God is holy (see 1 Peter 1:15–16). Human holiness is, of course, relative, not absolute. We are to remember that an unholy act will interrupt our fellowship with God (1 John 1:5–7), during which time there can be no assurance of answered prayer. Hypocrisy in our approach to God is condemned by His holiness (Matthew 6:1–7). If we know that God is holy and demands holiness of His creatures, then we are under serious obligation to put away all unholy thoughts and deeds.

Such a vision of God and His holiness will awaken within us a sense of our own sin and unworthiness. We will not be claiming sinless perfection. There will be, on the contrary, a growing sense of our own sin and worthlessness (1 John 1:7–8, 10). There will also be a feeling and attitude of reverence in our approach to and our behavior in the house of God.

God is loving, merciful, and gracious.
"God is love" (1 John 4:8).
"The Lord God, merciful and gracious, longsuffering, and abounding in goodness and truth" (Exodus 34:6).

Just as God is *light* (1 John 1:5) and *Spirit* (John 4:24), He is *love*. These three words are wonderfully illustrative of the divine nature and being. Love is difficult if not impossible to define. From certain Scriptures, however, we may infer that the love of God means a constant and solicitous interest in the physical, moral, and spiritual well-being of His creatures, such as leads Him to make sacrifices beyond human comprehension in order to manifest that love (see Romans 5:6–8). The supreme manifestation of God's love to man lies in the gift of His only begotten Son to die for the sins of the world. The cross of Christ is the highest expression of the love of a holy God providing an atonement for the sins of a guilty and lost world. It is because of the love of God that pardon and forgiveness are possible.

Oh, the love that drew salvation's plan!
Oh, the grace that brought it down to man!

> Oh, the mighty gulf that God did span
> At Calvary!

As the prophet Isaiah wrote, "But You have lovingly delivered my soul from the pit of corruption" (Isaiah 38:17). In making "children of God" (1 John 3:1–2) of those who formerly were rebels (Romans 5:10), God displays His great love for man.

From the love of God springs His *mercy* and *lovingkindness* to undeserving sinners. God waits to be gracious to the unkind, unworthy, and ungrateful. It is because of the mercy and longsuffering of God that sinners were not long ago destroyed (2 Peter 3:9). The whole scheme of our redemption and its carrying out in fact springs from the matchless and unmerited mercy and favor of God. That salvation springs from His favor and grace is clearly stated by Paul: "For by grace you have been saved through faith, and that not of yourselves; it is the gift of God, not of works, lest anyone should boast" (Ephesians 2:8–9).

God is just.
"He is faithful and just" (1 John 1:9).

In a sense God's justice is a necessary outcome of His holiness, a demonstration of His divine dealings with mankind. Holiness has to do more particularly with the character of God Himself; justice with that character as expressed in God's dealings with men.

The justice and righteousness of God manifest themselves in the making and imposing on mankind of just and holy laws, in the executing of penalties for any infringement of those laws, and in the actual carrying out of the holy and divine purposes in the government of the universe. The justice of God is free from all caprice or passion, and is vindicative, not vindictive.

This attribute of God assures us that God is not "too good" to punish sin. The fate of fallen angels, of Sodom and Gomorrah, and of the antediluvians is sufficient proof of this statement. God will assuredly punish the wicked and reward the righteous.

The parable of the prodigal son (in Luke 15) cannot, by any fair interpretation, be made to teach that God is too good to punish sin. This parable does not cover the whole of the plan of salvation; indeed, it is a real question whether it has anything to do with salvation at all. Certainly, even while setting forth the divine mind and attitude towards a returning sinner, it has nothing to say as to the cost or method of providing pardon for the erring. The parable was spoken to show the scribes and Pharisees, who were murmuring because Christ was receiving sinners, that they ought to be rejoicing rather (Luke 15:1–2, 32). We should not press parables beyond the point of meaning indicated in the text or context.

Summing up, then, the things every Christian should believe about God, we would say, first, that, as to the existence of God, the Christian must believe that He actually exists, that God is a real entity; second, as to His nature, he must believe that God is all-powerful, all-seeing, all-wise, everywhere present, eternal, unchangeable; and that He is holy, loving, merciful, gracious, and just.

Such a God is our God, so worthy of our supreme trust and confidence. How rich is our heritage in God!

CHAPTER FOUR

JESUS: WHO HE IS

JESUS CHRIST IS CHRISTIANITY, for Christianity is primarily and fundamentally not a creed or set of doctrines but a person. A Christian is not one who accepts a certain formula of accepted truth so much as one who actually accepts the personal Christ as Savior and Lord. There can be no Christianity without Christ.

"If you take away the name of Buddha from Buddhism and remove the personal revealer entirely from his system; if you take away the personality of Mahomet [Muhammad] from [Islam], or the personality of Zoroaster from the religion of the Parsees, the entire doctrine of these religions would still be left intact," wrote Sinclair Paterson. "Their practical value, such as it is, would not be imperiled or lessened. But take away from Christianity the name and person of Jesus Christ and what have you left? Nothing! The whole substance and strength of the Christian faith centers in Jesus Christ." And Denney concluded: "The Christian faith and life is determined by the person and the work of Jesus Christ. Its convictions are convictions about Him. Its hopes are hopes which He has inspired and which it is for Him to fulfill. Its ideals are born of His teaching and life. Its strength is the strength of His spirit."

The importance of having right views concerning Jesus Christ is very evident, therefore, when viewed from the standpoint of the important place He holds in the religion that bears His name. We cannot be right in the rest unless we think rightly of Him. Names and sects and parties fall, but Jesus Christ is all in all. Our eternal salvation depends upon what we think of Him and what relation we sustain to Him (John 8:24; 17:3). Let us, therefore, seek to understand the things we should know about Him in order to be saved, to walk worthy of Him, and to serve Him acceptably.

Let us consider Jesus Christ from the standpoint of His person and then of His work.

THE HUMANITY OF JESUS CHRIST
Jesus Christ was a true man.
"The Man Christ Jesus" (1 Timothy 2:5).
"'Behold the Man!'" (John 19:5).

Jesus Christ came into the world as other children do—over the ever thorny way of a woman's pain and sorrow. He was born of the Virgin Mary (Matthew 1:18; Luke 1:34–35). He was "born of a woman" (Galatians 4:4). Thus, Jesus Christ submitted to the conditions of a human life and a human body. He became humanity's son by a human birth. He was named "Jesus," "Jesus of Nazareth," and "Son of Man" over eighty times. He is "the Man Christ Jesus."

Of course there is a *great mystery* connected with the birth of Christ into this world. The manner of His entrance into the human race was different from the long lists of births that are named before it. It was not ordinary, but extraordinary and supernatural. Jesus Christ had no earthly father. Joseph was His supposed father (Luke 3:23). The doctrine of the Virgin Birth need not stagger us. We are totally unable to unravel the mystery of our own birth, how much less that of the entrance of deity into humanity.

The story of the supernatural entrance of Christ into the world is in harmony with the supernatural life He lived (John 8:46) and with His miraculous exit from the world (Acts 1:9). No laws of heredity are sufficient to account for His generation. By a creative act, God broke through the chain of human generation and brought into the world a supernatural being.

Jesus Christ was subject to the same sinless infirmities as other men. "In all points tempted . . ., yet without sin" (Hebrews 4:15).

As a child, Jesus grew as other children grow. He learned the things of God as other children learn them, by the teaching of His parents, and by His faithful attendance upon the services of the house of God (Luke 2:41). Just to what extent the sinless nature of Christ and His deity influenced such growth and progress we may not be able exactly to say, but we do know that Jesus grew and "increased in wisdom and stature, and in favor with God and men" (Luke 2:52). The self-emptying, while not consisting of the emptying of His deity, yet surely had reference to some voluntary self-limiting which affected His humanity.

It is incredible to think that, although possessing the divine attributes, Jesus should have held them in subjection in order that the Holy Spirit might have His part to play in that truly human and yet perfectly divine life (see Acts 10:38).

Jesus suffered from hunger and thirst (Matthew 4:2; John 19:28). He was subject to human weariness, and He slept (John 4:6; Matthew 8:24). He endured and suffered bodily pain, even unto death, as other human beings. Even from the standpoint of His purely human nature, He was sinless and He found it impossible to yield to sin. Yet He "suffered, being tempted" (Hebrews 2:18). The temptations, not only in the wilderness but all through His earthly life (Luke 4:13), were no sham or farce. They were real temptations, causing the Son of Man suffering.

Jesus Christ had every appearance of a man.
"'For in pouring this fragrant oil on My body, she did it for My burial'" (Matthew 26:12).

To the woman of Samaria, as well as to Mary Magdalene and the disciples on the way to Emmaus and out on the sea toiling fruitlessly all night, Jesus had all the appearance of a real man. He was "flesh and blood" (Hebrews 2:14), "became flesh" (John 1:14), possessed a "body" (Luke 24:39–40), "soul" (Matthew 26:38), and "spirit" (Luke 23:46); He had "hands and feet" (24:39).

By His incarnation, Jesus Christ came into the possession of a real human nature. He came not only to His own, but He came to them in the likeness of their own flesh. Of course, we must carefully distinguish between a human nature and a carnal nature. Christ's human nature was truly human but sinless—"without sin" (Hebrews 4:15). He was *a* son of man, but also *the* Son of Man.

What a comfort to us to know that He who was actual God was in reality human, bone of our bone and flesh of our flesh. "Inasmuch then as the children have partaken of flesh and blood, He Himself likewise shared in the same" (Hebrews 2:14). There is not a note in the great organ of our humanity which, when touched, does not find a sympathetic response in the mighty range and scope of the Savior's being—except, of course, the jarring discord of sin. Are we hungry, thirsty, weary, disappointed, misunderstood, maligned, persecuted, beaten, betrayed? So was He, and in a far deeper sense than we can ever be. We have not yet "resisted unto blood." But He did, and that for our sakes. And it is this very Son of Man, this one, who for us men and our salvation became man, who is to be our judge in that great day. How safe will be our interests in His hands! He has been appointed Judge "because He is the Son of Man" (John 5:27), because He fully understands all our trials and temptations, for He Himself has "suffered, being tempted" (Hebrews 2:18).

THE DEITY OF OUR LORD JESUS CHRIST

Jesus Christ was not only true man but God also. He was both divine and human; fully man, fully God. In Jesus of Nazareth dwelt "all the fullness of the Godhead bodily" (Colossians 2:9). He was not merely "godlike"; He was actually God. His name was "Immanuel," which means "God with us" (Matthew 1:23).

The Scriptures assert that Jesus Christ is God.
"In the beginning was the Word, and the Word was with God, and the Word was God" (John 1:1).
"Our great God and Savior Jesus Christ" (Titus 2:13).

Over and over again in the Scriptures, the name *God* is ascribed to Christ. "The Word was God." "But to the Son He says: 'Your throne, O God, is forever" (Hebrews 1:8). "We are in Him who is true, in His Son Jesus Christ. This is the true God" (1 John 5:20). We are aware that it is argued that absolute deity is not hereby proven, for human judges are "called gods" (John 10:35). True, but such are called "gods" in the relative sense, never in the absolute sense as in the references to Jesus Christ. The words of Thomas, "My Lord and my God!" are not to be considered a mere expression of amazement, but a confession of faith—a confession that Jesus positively accepted as being absolutely true, as His words that follow clearly show.

The Scriptures call Christ "the Son of God".
"'Truly You are the Son of God'" (Matthew 14:33).

Too numerous to record here are the Scriptures referring to this name. A few chosen passages are Matthew 8:29; 14:33; 16:16–17; Mark 1:1; Luke 1:35.

This title was not only claimed for Him by others, but by Jesus Himself: "For He said, 'I am the Son of God'" (Matthew 27:43). He declared the name before the high priest: "The high priest asked Him, saying to Him, 'Are You the Christ, the Son of the Blessed?' Jesus said, 'I am. And you will see the Son of Man sitting at the right hand of the Power, and coming with the clouds of heaven'" (Mark 14:61–62; see also John 10:36). Without any equivocation Jesus openly announced Himself as such (John 5:25; 11:4). Three times in the Gospels the Jews attempted to kill Christ, and in each instance it was because He claimed deity (John 5:18; 8:58–59; 19:7). Indeed it was for just such a claim that they finally slew Him (Matthew 26:62–66).

By the title "Son of God" a unique relation to God was clearly intended. The Jews would not stone one of their number simply for claiming that he was a son of God, for every Jew acknowledged that God was his Father. The claim Jesus here made was much more than that; it was unique; it was a claim that no mere human being had a right to make, a claim which in itself constituted blasphemy: "For a good work we do not stone You, but for blasphemy, and because You, being a Man, make Yourself God" (John 10:33).

It is totally fallacious to say that Jesus Christ was a son of God in the sense that "all men are sons of God, only, of course, that He was much more Godlike than any other of the sons of men." Scripture calls Him the "only begotten Son " (John 1:14, 18; 3:16, for example). The term *only begotten* means "the only one" (cf. "the only son of his mother," Luke 7:12; "for he is my only child," Luke 9:38; and "still having one son, his beloved," Mark 12:6). Note the contrast between the many "children of God" and "the only begotten Son" in John 1:12 and 18. We "become" sons of God by faith in Jesus Christ; Jesus Christ never "became" but always "was" the Son of God. We become children of God in time; He is Son of God from all eternity. He is Son of God by nature; we, by grace and adoption.

The Scriptures call Jesus Christ "Lord."
"'For there is born to you this day in the city of David a Savior, who is Christ the Lord'" (Luke 2:11).

It is remarkable to note that the translators of the Septuagint, when they came to the Hebrew word indicating Jehovah, translated it "Lord" (*kurios*), which always refers to that ineffable name of the divine Being (Jehovah), which, because of their reverence, they were afraid to write and pronounce. When, therefore, Jesus Christ is called "Lord," it is a clear testimony to the fact that He is deity, equal with Jehovah.

Such divine names as "First and Last" and "Alpha and Omega" in Revelation 22:13 show Jesus' preeminence. Interestingly, the phrase "I am the First and I am the Last" is the name of Jehovah in Isaiah 44:6; and "Alpha and Omega" in Revelation 1:8 is the name of "the Lord, . . . the Almighty." And in Acts 3:14, Jesus is called "the Holy One," the name the Lord gives Himself in Isaiah 43:3. In more than a score of times in Isaiah's prophecy, Jehovah Himself is called "the Holy One."

At least twelve other divine names are ascribed to Christ in the Scriptures, which we have not space here to treat. The names we have dealt with, however, are sufficient to prove that Jesus Christ is deity, viewed from the standpoint of divine names and titles.

Jesus Christ is to be worshipped even as God is worshipped.
"'That all should honor the Son just as they honor the Father'" (John 5:23).
"Let all the angels of God worship Him" (Hebrews 1:6).

The gifted poet Robert Browning once quoted, in a letter to a lady in her last illness, the words of Charles Lamb. Lamb, a fellow poet, had become light with some friends as to how he and they would feel if the greatest of the dead were to appear suddenly in flesh and blood once more. Then a friend asked how they would feel "if Christ entered this room?" Lamb changed his tone at once and stuttered out, as his manner was when moved, "You see . . . if Shakespeare entered, we should all rise. If Christ appeared, we must all kneel."

Deity, God alone, is to be worshipped. If then it is proper to render worship to Jesus Christ, He must be God. It is not enough to admire Christ; He demands, and the Father demands for Him, the worship of men and angels. God has "highly exalted Him and given Him the name which is above every name, that at the name of Jesus every knee should bow" (Philippians 2:9–10). But such homage would be a sacrilege if Christ were not God. "You shall worship the Lord your God, and Him only you shall serve" (Matthew 4:10).

Jesus accepted such worship as being properly due Him (Luke 24:52). Upon His great entry into Jerusalem to shouts of praise, objections from the Pharisees brought Jesus' remarkable reply, "I tell you that if these [disciples] should keep silent, the stones would immediately cry out" (Luke 19:40). It is worthy of note that the apostles refused such worship (Acts 14:13–15; 10:2–26). Even angels refused to permit men to worship them (Revelation 22:8–9). Who then was Christ, if not God, to unhesitatingly accept the worship of men as His proper due? Jesus Christ was either God, or He was an imposter. But His whole life refutes the idea of imposture.

As Stephen (Acts 7:59) and Paul (2 Corinthians 12:8–10) and the early Christians (1 Corinthians 1:2) called upon the Lord Jesus in prayer and worship, so should we. Let us not commit the awful sin of refusing to offer to Christ that which is His due (Psalm 2:12).

Attributes which belong to deity alone are ascribed to Jesus Christ, including preexistence, creation, and forgiveness of sins. "'Before Abraham was, I am'" (John 8:58).

He claimed preexistence and to be the source of all existence. In addressing the Father, He spoke of the glory which He had with Him "before the world was" (John 17:5). He maintained that the Father loved Him "before the foundation of the world" (17:24). The Word was in the beginning with God (see John 1:1).

The life of all men, whether physical life or the resurrection of spiritual life, is derived from Christ— He is its source (John 5:21, 26; 14:6; 11:25). He is eternal and unchangeable, even as God. "Jesus Christ is the same yesterday, today, and forever," the Scripture notes (Hebrews 13:8). Nature, men, and things change; He abides the same.

The Scriptures attribute to Jesus Christ the creation and preservation of all things. "All things were made through

Him, and without Him nothing was made that was made" (John 1:3). "In Him all things consist"; He is the upholder of them all (Colossians 1:17; Hebrews 1:3). The things in the universe do not happen haphazardly. Christ governs and controls. Was that why Paul could say, "We know that all things work together for good to those who love God" (Romans 8:28)? He well knew that Christ, his Lord and Savior, was at the helm of the universe. Nero might well say, "All things conspire against me"; Paul could say, "All things are working for my good."

Jesus claimed the right to forgive the sins of men (Mark 2:5–10; Luke 7:48), and the forgiveness of sins is an exclusively divine prerogative. No wonder the scribes and Pharisees accused Him of blasphemy in thus assuming to Himself a right that belonged to God alone. Christ not merely declared that sins were forgiven, as a minister might do as representing God; He actually forgave men their sins. He looked upon sin as an act committed against Himself, a fact well illustrated in the parable of the two debtors (Luke 7:39–50).

Resurrection and judgment are claimed as the prerogatives of the Son of God. Not the Father, but the Son is to be the judge of all men (John 5:22; 2 Timothy 4:1). It is at the sound of the voice of the Son of God that the dead come forth out of their graves (John 5:28–29; 11:43).

The divine attributes of omnipotence (Matthew 28:18), omniscience (John 16:30; Colossians 2:3), and omnipresence (Matthew 18:20; 28:20) are ascribed to Jesus Christ. What power He had in heaven and in earth! Nature (John 2:1–11), disease (Luke 4:38–41), death (John 11:43), demons (Luke 4:35), indeed "all things" (Hebrews 2:8) were under His control. "What a wonderful Saviour is Jesus, my Lord!" What marvelous knowledge He possessed of the inner thoughts (Mark 2:8), plans (John 13:21), and acts of men (Matthew 21:1–3; 16:21)! To Him the great panorama of the ages was as an open book (Matthew 24, 25). Past, present, and future were well-known to Him. Wherever His people met, there He was in their midst. Distance is no barrier to His personal presence. He fills all things and every place (Ephesians 1:23).

Surely, from the consideration of all these things, there should be no room for honest doubt concerning the fact Jesus Christ was actually divine. No one could possess all these divine prerogatives and not be actually God. My soul, thou hast made no mistake when thou didst lean upon Jesus Christ for thy salvation! No mere human, self-appointed, self-commissioned redeemer is He. All the power, wisdom, and knowledge of the Godhead dwells in Him. He upon whom you call for forgiveness and pardon will not leave until He has brought you into His banqueting house and spread His banner of love over you. "He who has begun a good work in you will complete it" (Philippians 1:6).

CHAPTER FIVE

JESUS:
WHAT HE DID

*G*OD DEALS WITH PEOPLE in this dispensation through the redemptive work of His Son, Jesus Christ. This is the sum and substance of the New Testament, or, better, the New Covenant. When Jesus was observing the Last Supper in the Upper Room, He said to the disciples, as He handed them the wine to drink, "This cup is the new covenant in My blood" (Luke 22:20). A covenant is an agreement, a method of dealing with others. God saw fit to establish a covenant between Himself and His creatures. According to the New Covenant, then, God has redemptive dealings with men during this age only on the basis of the shed blood of His Son Jesus Christ.

THE REDEMPTIVE WORK OF JESUS CHRIST

How vital then for us, who stand in such great need of the benefits of grace such as pardon, peace, power, sanctification, and glorification, to understand and appreciate, as fully as we may, the redemptive work of our Lord Jesus.

The Death of Jesus Christ.
"Christ died for our sins" (1 Corinthians 15:3).
"Our Lord Jesus Christ . . . gave Himself for our sins" (Galatians 1:3–4).

The death of Christ is vital to Christianity. Other great men have been valued for their lives. Jesus Christ wished to be remembered by His death: "Do this in remembrance of Me" were the words He uttered as He passed the communion cup to the disciples. A memorial of His death was His parting gift to them. Christianity is more than ethical; it is redemptive. Indeed, it cannot be ethical unless it is first redemptive. The Cross is the magnet and power of Christian living (Galatians 6:14; 1 Peter 2:24).

WRONG VIEWS ABOUT CHRIST'S DEATH

Many and various are the views held concerning the death of our Lord and Savior Jesus Christ. Many, alas, are totally unscriptural and therefore untrue. Let us glance briefly at some of the erroneous views of the death of Christ—*modern views of the atonement* they are called. Well, perhaps we need to be reminded that "what is new is not true, and what is true is not new."

Christ's death is looked upon by some as *an accident*, something unforeseen by Christ, and not in the plan of God. But Jesus knew all about it and foretold it long before it happened (Matthew 16:21; Mark 9:30–32). Jesus voluntarily laid down His life; it was not snatched from Him (John 10:17–18). He knew all about the plots and plans of His enemies. He well knew, too, that He had come to fulfill the Old Testament Scriptures that clearly portrayed His death (Matthew 26:54; Luke 24:27, 44).

Others look upon the death of Christ as *the death of a martyr*, like that of Polycarp, or Savonarola. But neither Jesus nor any of the writers of the New Testament so spoke of it. Paul had seen Stephen the martyr die, but he never associated forgiveness of sins with his death. Why, if Jesus died as a martyr, was He seemingly denied the presence of God in His last moments (Matthew 27:46), whereas other martyrs have had their last moments flooded with the sunshine of the divine presence? Can Christ's conduct in the Garden of Gethsemane be explained on any other basis than that He was there as the bearer of the world's load of sin, which was crushing out His life? Was He a brave martyr if that is all He was? How does His apparent cringing (Luke 22:39–46) compare with the manifest heroism and bravery of many other martyrs?

Still others look upon Christ's death as being for the purpose of setting forth a great *moral example*. The sight of such suffering is intended to soften and win human hearts and to lead them to a better life. But does it? Do not men look the suffering Christ in the face and go deliberately sinning? Those who are softened and won by it do so because they realize that that suffering was for their sin, and that, in that death, they have life.

It is difficult to see how any so-called *governmental theory* of Christ's death can satisfy the facts in the case. Surely if God had to make an example of His great wrath against sin, it was hardly necessary that He should vent that wrath on the purest and sweetest man that ever lived. Why bring into the world a supernatural being, as Christ was, for such a purpose? Were there not enough men already in the world who were sinful enough to merit just such punishment? Why punish the innocent and not the guilty? Is that a good example of government?

THE RIGHT MEANING OF CHRIST'S DEATH

We can readily see that the modern mind fails to find in the death of Christ what the orthodox faith holds as essential to its true nature and purpose. The Scriptures set forth the death of Christ in a fourfold manner:

First, His death is considered *a ransom:* "The Son of Man [came] . . . to give His life a ransom for many" (Matthew 20:28). By a ransom is meant the price paid for the buying back of a person or thing. Man had sold himself to sin and Satan. Christ, by His death, paid the price which redeemed man from such bondage. As Peter wrote, we were "redeemed . . . with the precious blood of Christ" (1 Peter 1:18–19).

Second, Christ's death is *a propitiation* (Romans 3:25; 1 John 2:2). The lid or covering of the ark of the covenant, which contained the Ten Commandments, and on which the blood of the sacrificed lamb was sprinkled by the high priest in order to atone for the sins against God and His holy law, was called "the mercy seat" or "propitiation." It was the place where God met the interceding high priest and received the blood of atonement by virtue of which He granted pardon to the sinful and sinning nation. So the death of Jesus Christ is the place where, and the ground on which, a holy God can grant pardon to sinful and sinning mankind. There God meets the sinner, and, on the ground of atoning blood, pardons and receives him into favor.

Third, Christ's death is looked upon as *a reconciliation* (Romans 5:10; 2 Corinthians 5:18–19; Colossians 1:20). Sin erected a barrier between God and man; it created an enmity between them. Fellowship between God and man was impossible because of sin and remained so until some means had been devised to remove sin, which was the ground of the existing enmity (Romans 8:7). Now the death of Jesus Christ is the ground on which such enmity can be removed. Calvary removes, or makes possible by faith the removal of, the barrier and the estrangement. God and man are friends by reason of the death of Christ—that is to say, such a friendship by relationship is possible, and actually takes place, when man accepts God's way of atonement.

Fourth, the death of Christ is *a substitution* (Isaiah 53:4–6; 2 Corinthians 5:21; 1 Peter 2:24). In these passages the actual word *substitution* is not found, but the idea certainly is. It is clearly taught that Jesus Christ, the righteous One, took the place of man, the sinner; that "He made Him who knew no sin to be sin for us," in order that we, who had no righteousness, "might become the righteousness of God in Him." Surely this means that Christ took our place. That is substitution. He gave Himself "for" (and that means "instead of") us and our sins.

ATONEMENT FOR OUR SINS

The necessity for the death of Christ lay in a twofold fact: God is holy; we are sinful. There can be no true understanding of the atonement unless these two related facts are seen in their true light. Light views of either the holiness of God or the exceeding sinfulness of man will not see much necessity for such a transaction as that which took place at Calvary.

God is absolutely holy (see page 73). No sinner can for a moment stand in His presence, much less abide with Him eternally, so long as sin remains on, with, and in the sinner, and has not in some way been atoned for, punished, and removed. Only then is it possible for a holy God to be righteous and at the same time pardon the sinner and treat him as though he had not sinned. "Being justified freely by His grace through the redemption that is in Christ Jesus, whom God set forth as a propitiation by His blood, through faith, to demonstrate His righteousness, because in His forbearance God has passed over the sins that were previously committed, to demonstrate at the present time His righteousness, that He might be just and the justifier of the one who has faith in Jesus" (Romans 3:24–26).

The Cross of Christ was a practical demonstration or exhibition as to the seriousness with which God views sin. It was by no means a light, trivial thing. It stood as an eternal barrier between God and man. Nothing but the death of Christ could, in the estimation of God, remove that barrier. The absolutely holy nature of God and His righteousness is not now, because of the death of Christ, compromised, even though He does receive the repentant and believing sinner into fellowship with Himself.

Thus the death of Christ as a complete atonement for sin becomes *sufficient* for the whole world (John 1:29; 1 John 2:2), and *efficient* for everyone who believes on Jesus (Acts 13:38–39; 1 Timothy 4:10). There is not a sinner in the whole world, however "weak," "without strength," "ungodly" (Romans 5:6–8), or "lost" (Luke 19:10) he may be, who may not be a partaker of the benefits of Christ's death. Even the "chief of sinners" may find perfect salvation in God's wondrous provision (1 Timothy 1:15–16).

Jesus Christ "tasted death for every man" (Hebrews 2:9) so that every man may say, "He loved me and gave Himself for me" (Galatians 2:20). When this particular phase of the atonement first dawned upon Martin Luther, the great reformer, he was found sobbing beneath a crucifix, moaning: "Mein Gott! Mein Gott! Fur Mich! Fur Mich!" ("My God! My God! For me! For me!").

"The wages of sin is death," Paul wrote (Romans 6:23). Christ came into the world in order that through dying He might pay the debt and free man from its awful burden (Hebrews 2:14). Christ was speaking of His death in its relation to the overthrow of Satan's power and kingdom when He said: "'Now is the judgment of this world; now the ruler of this world will be cast out. And I, if I am lifted up from the earth, will draw all peoples to Myself.' This He said, signifying by what death He would die" (John 12:31–33).

The sin question is no longer an unsettled question. Jesus Christ settled it once and for all on the cross. That God was satisfied with that settlement of the sin question is evident from the fact that He raised

Christ from the dead and exalted Him to His own right hand (Acts 2:32–33; Philippians 2:5–10). The paramount question confronting man today is the question: "What do you think of Christ?" "What then shall I do with Jesus who is called Christ?" The issues of eternity are determined by one's answer to and attitude towards that question (John 8:21, 24). "For judgment (crisis) I have come into this world" (John 9:39).

THE RESURRECTION OF JESUS CHRIST
The Resurrection shows Jesus is the Son of God.
"His Son Jesus Christ Our Lord, . . . declared to be the Son of God with power, . . . by the resurrection from the dead" (Romans 1:3–4).

The resurrection of Jesus Christ from the dead "the third day according to the Scriptures" (1 Corinthians 15:4) had a most vital relation to His redemptive death. Had the body of Christ remained in the tomb beyond the divinely appointed time of three days and three nights; had the physical form of Jesus been permitted to "see corruption" (Acts 2:31); had it remained in that tomb in Joseph's garden until the "resurrection at the last day" (John 11:24)—then we would have had no proof that the Father was pleased with the sacrifice which the Son had made upon the cross, nor would we have had the assurance of pardon and forgiveness through the redemptive work of Jesus Christ.

The raising of Jesus from the dead was the seal of the Father's approval on the work of His Son in connection with the offering of His life as an atonement for sin. The resurrection was the Father's "Amen!" to the Son's "It is finished!"

The resurrection of Jesus Christ from the dead "declared" Him to be, set Him apart from all the other sons of men as, "the Son of God" (Romans 1:4). It did not "make" but "declared" Him to be the Son of God.

Again and again in His ministry Christ was challenged as to His authority for His acts and teachings. He appealed to His resurrection as proof of His claims to deity and as sufficient guarantee as to the authority of His teachings (see Matthew 12:38–42; John 2:18–22). It was impossible that Jesus, spotless and sinless as He was, laying claims to divine prerogatives as He did, and appealing again and again as He did to His resurrection from the death as proof of the truth of it all—it was impossible that God should allow Him to have remained in the grave. To have done so would have been to give the lie to all the claims of His Son, and to leave the world in doubt as to any saving efficacy that might have attached itself to His death on the cross. As Peter declared during his sermon during Pentecost, "Whom God raised up, having loosed the pains of death, because it was not possible that He should be held by it" (Acts 2:24).

The believer in Christ may rest perfectly assured that all his sins which were laid on Jesus are entirely removed, pardoned, and forgiven. God was perfectly satisfied with the sacrifice for our sins which His Son made. The empty tomb in Joseph's garden on that first Easter morn proclaimed to us the comforting news of pardon and justification. We who believe on the Son are forgiven of all things (Acts 13:38–39).

The Resurrection gives those who believe a High Priest in heaven. "Seeing then that we have a great High Priest who has passed through the heavens, Jesus the Son of God, let us hold fast our confession" (Hebrews 4:14).

The resurrection of Jesus Christ gives to the believer *an interceding High Priest in heaven* (Hebrews 7:25–26; Romans 8:34). Immediately after His ascension, Christ took His place at the right hand of the Father, there to intercede for the believer. Satan is the "accuser of the brethren" (Revelation 12:10); whenever a child of God sins, Satan stands there in the presence of God (see Job 1 and 2) ready to accuse him and to demand the execution of the sentence against sin. It is then that our Savior pleads for us by virtue of the nail-scarred hands and feet and spear-thrust side. Jesus pleads His death and the Father's acceptance of such by raising Him from the dead as the ground for pardon and remittance of penalty for sins for all who believe. Our temporary falls after we have accepted Jesus as our Savior do not mar our relationship with God the Father. "We have an Advocate with the Father, Jesus

Christ the righteous" (1 John 2:1). His plea for us never fails. The Savior Himself said, "I know that You always hear Me " (John 11:42).

As the High Priest, Jesus is seated in heaven at "the right hand of God." This is the place of power. Christ has been exalted to that place by the Father. "The exceeding greatness of His power . . . which He worked in Christ when He raised Him from the dead and seated Him at His right hand in the heavenly places, far above all principality and power and might . . . and gave Him to be head over all things to the church" (Ephesians 1:19–22). All the power of the universe is in the hands of the Savior, and it is there at and for the disposal of the believer; it is "power toward us who believe" (verse 19).

No sin in life is beyond His power to conquer; no weakness cannot be offset by His strength, no failure that need not have been victory in His might. Nor is any virtue unattainable when He is looked to for power to realize it. No scheme of Satan or wile of demon can prevail if we look to Him to whom all principalities and powers are subject.

Oh, believer in Christ, look to the risen, ascended, and glorified Christ, and "nothing shall be impossible to you!" Jesus has said, "All authority has been given to Me in heaven and on earth" (Matthew 28:18).

The Resurrection guarantees our resurrection.
"'Because I live, you will live also'" (John 14:19).

There is one comforting thought that should not be overlooked in connection with the resurrection of our Lord Jesus from the dead: Our own resurrection from the dead is absolutely guaranteed by His. "For if we believe that Jesus died and rose again, even so God will bring with Him those who sleep in Jesus" (1 Thessalonians 4:14). As empty as was the tomb in Joseph's garden on that first Easter morn twenty centuries ago will be every believer's grave in that morn when the trumpet shall sound and the dead in Christ shall rise triumphant. They shall triumph over death and the grave to enjoy immortality and eternal bliss.

What a glorious hope! Think of all that is wrapped up in those blessed words: "Because I live, you will live also." It means not only the raising and glorifying of our own bodies, but also those of our loved ones whom "we have loved long since and lost awhile." What a meeting that will be! What a gathering of the saints from the north, south, east, and west, to sit down with the loved ones in the kingdom of the Father!

Of course, the wicked, too, are raised from the dead at the sound of His voice, but their resurrection is to eternal death, not to life everlasting (John 5:24–29). Indeed, there is a sad aspect of the resurrection of Jesus Christ. The resurrection of Christ is a proof positive and sufficient to all men as to *the certainty of a coming judgment day*. Someday the wicked and unbelieving, those who have refused to believe in Christ even in the face of overwhelming proof of the truth of His claims—as evidenced by His resurrection from the dead—will have to stand before God and answer for such unbelief. "Because He has appointed a day on which He will judge the world in righteousness by the Man whom He has ordained. He has given assurance [literally "faith" or "proof"] of this to all by raising Him from the dead" (Acts 17:31).

THE RETURN OF OUR LORD JESUS CHRIST
Jesus Christ will come again to earth.
"For the Lord Himself will descend from heaven with a shout, with the voice of an archangel, and with the trumpet of God" (1 Thessalonians 4:16).

Jesus Christ will return to earth. The importance of a right understanding of this doctrine can hardly be overestimated. Whereas the first coming of Christ is mentioned once in the Scriptures, His second coming is mentioned eight times. One out of every twenty-five verses in the New Testament is said to be devoted to its teaching; 318 references to it are found in the 216 chapters. The prophets of the Old Testament (1 Peter 1:10–11), angels (Acts 1:11), Jesus Himself (Matthew 24–25; John 14:3), as well as the apostles of the Lord Jesus (Acts 3:19–21; 1 Thessalonians 4:14–18; Hebrews 9:28), all bear witness to the great doctrine of the coming again to this world of Jesus Christ. Such a hope is set forth as a great incentive to Christian living (1 John 3:3; Luke 21:34–36), as the forward look of hope for the church of Christ (Titus 2:13), and as the greatest solace of the believer during his earthly life (1 Thessalonians 4:14–18).

Just why the doctrine of our Lord's coming again should not be proclaimed more than it is surpasses the comprehension of the thorough Bible student who sees this grand and glorious doctrine on almost every page of his Bible. Watching, working, waiting for the coming of our great God and Savior Jesus Christ ought to be the characteristic pose of every believer.

Christ's second coming will be personal and visible.
"This same Jesus, who was taken up from you into heaven, will so come in like manner as you saw Him go into heaven" (Acts 1:11).

When we speak of the coming again of our Lord, we mean His *personal, visible, bodily coming again* to this earth, not in humiliation as at the first advent (Philippians 2:5–8), to suffer and to die for the sins of mankind (1 John 3:5), but to reign in glory and to take to Himself the kingdoms of this world. "So Christ was offered once to bear the sins of many. To those who eagerly wait for Him He will appear a second time, apart from sin, for salvation" (Hebrews 9:28).

Pentecost may be looked upon as *a*, but surely not *the*, coming again of Christ. Nor was the destruction of Jerusalem, closely resembling the Second Coming as it did in so many points, the fulfillment of that predicted event. Nor yet are we to look upon death itself as the coming of Christ, for in death the believer goes to be with Christ rather than that Christ comes for him. One has but to note particularly the events that, in Scripture, are associated with the coming again of Christ, such as the raising of the righteous dead and the changing of the bodies of the righteous living, etc., to be convinced that no such things occurred at Pentecost or the destruction of Jerusalem, nor do they occur at the death of the believer. The coming again of Jesus Christ is an event predicted in the Scriptures which is still future, and for the fulfillment of which, with longing and anxious hearts, we still look.

The date of Christ's return is unknown but imminent.
"'But of that day and hour no one knows, not even the angels of heaven, but My Father only'"(Matthew 24:36).

Just when this great event shall take place no one knows. No man knows either the day or the hour (Matthew 24:36–42). Those who would set a specific date for the coming of our Lord thereby discredit themselves as reliable expositors of the Word of God. "But of that day and hour no one knows, . . . but My Father only," said Jesus. And before His ascension to heaven, He repeated the caution: "It is not for you to know times or the seasons which the Father has put in

His own authority" (Acts 1:7). In the face of such statements as these, why dare any man set a date for our Lord's coming? "For the Son of Man is coming at an hour you do not expect."

Of course, it is possible for us to know that *it is imminent.* The Master Himself gave certain signs that indicate the near approach of His coming (Matthew 24:36–42; compare also 1 Thessalonians 5:1–5). We should remember also in this connection that at least two great events comprise the coming again of our Lord: His coming *for* the saints (1 Thessalonians 4:14–17; 1 Corinthians 15:50–53), and His coming *with* them (Jude 14–15; compare Revelation 19:11–16). His coming *for* the saints is an event which may take place *at any moment.* Certain specific events must take place before the coming *with* the saints—such events as the Seventieth Week, the Great Tribulation (Daniel 9:25–27; Matthew 24:29).

WHEN CHRIST COMES

We are not left in ignorance as to what Christ is going to do when He comes again. We may not know everything about it, but we know some things.

The righteous dead will rise first.
"For the Lord Himself will descend from heaven with a shout, . . . and the dead in Christ will rise first" (1 Thessalonians 4:16).

First, Christ will raise the righteous dead. Not all the dead, however. "The rest of the dead did not live again until the thousand years were finished" (Revelation 20:5; cf. 1 Corinthians 15:23–24). When Jesus comes again, the grave of every believer will empty. Like Lazarus, they shall hear His voice and come forth.

Believers rest in hope. We shall sleep but not forever; there shall be a glorious dawn. The body of that loved one whose eyes you may have closed in death will awaken in that morn and see the King in His beauty in the land that is not far off. What a wonderful sight that will be to see graves, tombs, and mausoleums overturned and the dead in Christ coming forth triumphant over death!

The saints will receive transformed bodies.
"We shall not all sleep (die), but we shall all be changed" (1 Corinthians 15:51).

Second, Christ will change the bodies of the righteous living when He comes again. "Flesh and blood cannot inherit the kingdom of God" (1 Corinthians 15:50). These bodies of our humiliation are to be transformed into the likeness of the body of His glory (Philippians 3:21). No more sickness, no more bodies racked with pain, no more need of spectacles or crutches, no more physical infirmity, no more longing for the coming of the morn because of pain almost unbearable. All that will be changed in a moment, in the twinkling of an eye.

> Soon will our Saviour from heaven appear;
> Sweet is the hope and its power to cheer;
> All will be changed by a glimpse of His face;
> This is the goal at the end of our race.

The saints will receive their reward when the Lord comes.
"For we must all appear before the judgment seat of Christ, that each one may receive the things done in the body, according to what he has done, whether good or bad" (2 Corinthians 5:10).

When Christ comes, we will appear at the judgment seat of Christ: This judgment will be of the works, not the salvation, of the believer. The moment a man believes in Christ the matter of his eternal salvation is settled once for all (John 5:24). It is never again brought into question. But the place he will have in the life to come will depend upon his faithfulness. Whether he shall rule over three, or five, or ten cities will depend upon the use he has made of the gifts and talents God has entrusted to him. The "judgment seat of Christ," then, is not a judgment regarding destiny, but for adjustment, for reward or loss according to works, for position in the new sphere of life. That the saints are those referred to as appearing in this judgment is clear from 2 Corinthians 5:1 and 1 Corinthians

4:5, where it is said that those who are thus judged shall have praise of God.

Not always is the believer rewarded in this life for all the good he does. "Light is sown for the righteous" (Psalm 97:11); it will bring forth its fullness of fruition in the life to come. That is a comforting thought for the believer. Often when we do a bit of good for God we are misunderstood, our motives are impugned, we are accused of selfishness and a host of other things. What a comfort to know that some day our blessed Lord will say, "Well done," and reward us for every bit of good we have done in His name and for His sake!

The Jews will receive justice.
"So again in these days I am determined to do good to Jerusalem and to the house of Judah" (Zechariah 8:15).

Christ is coming to deal again with the Jew. For many centuries the Jew has been cast off and the Gentiles seem to have entered into his inheritance. But "the times of the Gentiles" will not last forever. The chosen people of God will again come into their own. God has not cast off His people forever (Romans 11:1, 25–32). The Jews will be restored to their own land (Isaiah 11:11; 60), probably in an unconverted state; they are likely to rebuild the temple and restore worship (Ezekiel 40–43). They will enter into a covenant with the Antichrist, which will be broken and as a result they will pass through the Great Tribulation (Daniel 9:27; Matthew 24:21–22, 29; Revelation 7:14). Finally, as a nation, they will turn to their Messiah and become great missionaries (Zechariah 12:10; 8:13–23).

Christ will establish His millennial kingdom on earth.
"They . . . reigned with Christ for a thousand years" (Revelation 20:4).

Finally, Christ is coming again to set up His millennial reign on the earth (Revelation 20:1–4). During this period, Christ Himself is King (Jeremiah 23:5; Luke 1:30–33). Jerusalem will doubtless be the capital city, to which pilgrims will wend their way (Isaiah 2:1–2). It is likely that the apostles will reign over the Jews, and the church over the Gentiles (Isaiah 66; Matthew 19:28). Sin will then be as scarce as righteousness is now, and righteousness will then be as prevalent as sin is now. The reign of Christ will be one of equity and righteousness (Isaiah 11:4). Among the events following the Millennium are apostasy and rebellion (Revelation 20:7–9), the destruction of Satan (20:10), the great White Throne judgment (20:13, 15), and the new heavens and the new earth (21 and 22).

The five events here set forth by no means comprise every event connected with Christ's coming again to this earth. They are among the principal events of that time, and probably of deepest interest to us.

CHAPTER SIX

THE HOLY SPIRIT

THERE ARE THREE AGES of revelation within the Bible: the age of the Father, comprising the Old Testament; the age of the Son, as contained in the Gospels; and the age of the Holy Spirit, comprising the remainder of the New Testament. In the first age, God the Father is the prominent actor or executive; in the second, God the Son; in the third, God the Holy Spirit. We are living in the age of the Spirit, and it becomes us, therefore, to familiarize ourselves with the Holy Spirit: His nature, being, person, and work.

"We have not so much as heard whether there is a Holy Spirit," some disciples in Ephesus once told Paul (Acts 19:2). In this day, many Christians are in the same ignorant condition with reference to the Holy Spirit as were those Ephesian believers, who did not so much as know that there was any Holy Spirit or that He had been bestowed upon believers (see 19:1–7). In this primer of Christian doctrine, we can only point out those things, and those only briefly, that are considered most necessary for the Christian to know for holy living and effective service.

THE NATURE OF THE HOLY SPIRIT

The Holy Spirit is a Person.
"'However, when He, the Spirit of truth, has come, He will guide you into all truth'" (John 16:13).

Because the ministry and operations of the Spirit are of a somewhat more mystical and invisible nature than that of the Father—in the creation, for example—and that of the Son—in the incarnation and redemption—we are prone to look upon the Holy Spirit as less of a Person than either of the other Persons in the Godhead. We may also neglect the Spirit's personhood because the Spirit is spoken of in such symbolic and figurative expressions as wind, breath, fire, and oil. So much is said in the Scriptures of the influence, grace, and power of the Spirit that we may be led, unless we are careful, to look upon the third Person in the Trinity as a manifestation of the Father or the Son or of both, rather than as a Person distinct as Father or Son.

Our concept of the Holy Spirit as a Person or an influence has its effect upon our life and service. It is of great moment for me to know whether the Holy Spirit is an influence or power which I may use in my life and service for God, or whether He is a divine Person who is to use me as He sees fit in order that I may glorify the Father and the Son in my life and service. We can readily see then how vital it is for every Christian to know all he can about the Holy Spirit.

That the Holy Spirit is a Person is clear from the fact that *He takes the place of a Person*—Jesus Christ: "And I will pray the Father, and He will give you another Helper, that He may abide with you forever" (John 14:16). Only a person can take the place of a person. Jesus had announced His departure to His disciples. They were feeling sorrowful. So Jesus gave comfort by the assurance that the Helper ("Comforter" in the King James Version), which is the Holy Spirit, would take His place, and really do more for them than He Himself: "I still have many things to say to you, but you cannot bear them now. However, when He, the Spirit of truth, has come, He will guide you into all truth" (John 16:12–13).

For this reason also, *personal pronouns are used of the Holy Spirit.* No less than twelve times in John 16:7, 8, 13–15 is the pronoun "He" (Greek: *ekeinos*—"that one, He") used of the Holy Spirit. This is the same word that is used to describe Christ (cf. 1 John 2:6; 3:3, 5, 7, 16), whose place the Spirit takes. This is a fact of paramount importance when we remember that the Greek word for *spirit* is a neuter word and should have a neuter pronoun.

A careful consideration of the *Baptismal Formula* (Matthew 28:19), and the *Apostolic Benediction* (2 Corinthians 13:14), compels us to attribute personality to the Holy Spirit, even as to the Father and the Son. How foolish and irreverent it would be, for example, to say, "Go, baptize them in the name of the Father and of the Son and of the *wind* or *breath*."

The Holy Spirit possesses attributes of personality: He has *knowledge* (1 Corinthians 2:10–11). He *distributes* spiritual gifts (1 Corinthians 12). He has *will* and *mind* (1 Corinthians 12:11; Romans 8:27). He *speaks* (Revelation 2:7), *makes intercession* (Romans 8:26), *oversees* matters pertaining to the church (Acts 13:2). He may be *grieved* (Ephesians 4:30), *insulted* (Hebrews 10:29), *lied to* (Acts 5:3), and *blasphemed* and *sinned against* (Matthew 12:31–32).

What a wonderful truth lies in this phase of the doctrine of the Holy Spirit! And this is the truth that lies couched in the word "Helper," which is a (or perhaps the) name of the Spirit, meaning one whom we may call to our side in the time of trouble. Side by side He walked with the faithful in the early church; they were "walking . . . in the comfort of the Holy Spirit" (Acts 9:31).

The Holy Spirit is a Divine Person.
"'Why has Satan filled your heart to lie to the Holy

Spirit . . . ? You have lied not to men but to God'" (Acts 5:3–4).

In the Scripture quoted above, the Holy Spirit is distinctly called *God*. In 2 Corinthians, He is also called *Lord* (3:18), a name which, as we have already seen (p. 87), is a name of deity.

The Holy Spirit fully possesses attributes of deity. He is *omniscient*. He knows all things (1 Corinthians 2:10–11), and thus, knowing what is the mind of God and what is in our hearts, He is eminently fitted to be intercessor and pleader in our behalf (Romans 8:26). Indeed our prayers are true prayers only as they are inspired and composed by the Spirit of God; only then will our requests be "according to the will of God."

The Holy Spirit is omnipresent. He is everywhere (Psalm 139:7–10). But only God fills heaven, earth, and everywhere; therefore the Holy Spirit is God.

The Holy Spirit is omnipotent. "The power of the Highest" is His (Luke 1:35). The *creation* of all things is ascribed to the Spirit even as unto the Father and the Son (Genesis 1:2; Psalm 104:30). "The Spirit of God has made me, and the breath of the Almighty gives me life" (Job 33:4). The new and *spiritual creation* within the soul of man is the work of the Spirit (John 3:5–8), as is also *the resurrection* of the believer's body in that great day (Romans 8:11).

The Holy Spirit therefore is entitled to our *worship*. He is to be worshipped as God because He is actually

God. It is a sin to withhold worship from Him. It is true that the Scriptures do not as distinctly enjoin upon us the necessity of such worship as they do in the case of the Father and the Son. There is a reason for such silence. It is preeminently the work of the Holy Spirit to bear witness, not to Himself, but to Jesus Christ. It is His work to keep in the background, as it were, and to make Christ prominent. "He will glorify Me, for He will take of what is mine and declare it to you" (John 16:14).

THE RELATION OF THE HOLY SPIRIT
TO THE BELIEVER

It is exceedingly important for every Christian to know what relation he sustains to the Holy Spirit. Success in the Christian life in all its phases depends upon the Holy Spirit. Ignorance in this respect means certain defeat and failure.

Every Christian has the Holy Spirit.
"If anyone does not have the Spirit of Christ, he is not His" (Romans 8:9).

No man can come to the knowledge of Jesus Christ as Savior and the acceptance of Him as such unless the Spirit of God enables him so to do. "No one can say that Jesus is Lord except by the Holy Spirit" (1 Corinthians 12:3). His regeneration (John 3:3–5;

Titus 3:5) and articulation into the body of Christ as a member (1 Corinthians 12:13) is the distinctive work of God's Holy Spirit. He is the executive of the Godhead, and applies to the soul of man the work of redemption wrought by the Son and planned by the Father (see Ephesians 1:3–14).

It is erroneous, therefore, for Christians to pray that God would give them His Holy Spirit as though He were not already abiding in them, for He already possesses them; otherwise they are not children of God (Romans 8:9). The *fullness* of the Spirit they may not have, but His *indwelling* they most certainly have (1 Corinthians 6:19). At Pentecost the Holy Spirit came to abide with the believer and the church, and He has never left them since, nor will He, until that day when "He who now restrains . . . [will be] taken out of the way" (2 Thessalonians 2:7).

Every Christian does not have the fullness of the Holy Spirit. "Do not be drunk with wine . . . but be filled with the Spirit" (Ephesians 5:18).

Egypt always had the river Nile, but not always the overflow of the Nile. And yet on that overflow the harvests of Egypt depend. When the Nile overflows its banks, it leaves behind it a rich alluvial deposit that moistens and enriches the soil and makes an abundant harvest possible. No overflow means famine for Egypt. Just so is it with the Christian in his relation to the

Holy Spirit. He may have the Holy Spirit *indwelling*, but if he does not have the Spirit *infilling* and *overflowing*, his life will be barren of the graces, gifts, and fruit of the Spirit (Galatians 5:22–23).

To many believers, this specific experience of the infilling with the Holy Spirit comes some time after their conversion, too often after long years of wearisome defeat and failure in life and service. Then, oh glorious experience! This is the power for living the Christian life.

There is such a thing as "the law of the Spirit" (Romans 8:2). When we obey that law, even though it be the law of faith, we receive the fullness of the Spirit. "God has given [the Holy Spirit] to those who obey Him" (Acts 5:32). *Obedience* to the will and word of the Spirit is one of the conditions of being "filled with the Spirit." Are we, as far as we know from the Word of God (and are we diligently studying the Word of God to find out what His will is?), living up to the light we have received and gladly rendering full obedience? Disobedience to any known command will issue in a famine of the Spirit's power in life.

Jesus Christ must be *enthroned in the heart* and life if we are to enjoy the fullness of the Spirit's presence. "This He spoke concerning the Spirit, whom those believing in Him would receive; for the Holy Spirit was not yet given, because Jesus was not yet glorified" (John 7:39). By "the Spirit" here is meant the infilling and overflowing of the Spirit, as is clear from verses 37 and 38. If self rather than Christ is the ruler on the throne of our hearts, we cannot have the fullness of the Spirit. He came into the world to "glorify Christ" and Him alone. He will not give you power to run your own water mill.

Christ is the beginning, as Christ is the end of the Spirit-filled life. Is He of your life and mine?

Having the fullness of the Holy Spirit brings many positive results. "The law of the Spirit of life in Christ Jesus has made me free from the law of sin and death" (Romans 8:2).

Assurance of our personal salvation is a work of the Spirit in our hearts. "In whom also, having believed, you were sealed with the Holy Spirit of promise" (Ephesians 1:13). It is the Spirit Himself who "bears witness with our spirit that we are children of God" (Romans 8:16). It is not enough for a man to be saved; he should know he is saved (1 John 5:13). Yet how many Christians there are, real Christians too, who do not enjoy the blessing of assurance of salvation. They cannot be joyful because they are not sure that their "sins are forgiven" (1 John 2:12), that their names are written in the Lamb's Book of Life in heaven (Luke 10:20; Revelation 20:15), and that they are even now actual sons and daughters of God (John 1:12; 1 John 3:1–2). Thus Fanny Crosby could write:

Blessed assurance, Jesus is mine!
Oh, what a foretaste of glory divine!

Being filled with the Holy Spirit brings fullness of power in life and service (Acts 10:38). What a marked difference is discernible in the life and service of the apostles before and after Pentecost! What blunders Peter, for example, was continually making, and what a lack of power in testimony there was in his life before Pentecost: impulsive (Mark 14:47), headstrong and arbitrary (John 13:8), and cowardly, even denying that he ever knew his Master (Matthew 26:34–35, 69–75)! Yet what a tremendous contrast after the Holy Spirit had fallen on him! What calm, poise, courage, boldness, sacrifice was exhibited in his whole life after the outpouring of the Holy Spirit! Read carefully the account of his ministry in Acts 2–12, especially chapters 2–5, and note the change. And just this difference will be made in the lives of all who receive of His fullness.

Being filled with the Holy Spirit also brings victory over sin. What a deep groan of defeat and hopeless failure issues from the seventh chapter of Romans! And why? Read it carefully and note, as you read it, that the Holy Spirit is not once mentioned in the chapter. What a paeon of triumphant victory issues forth from the eighth chapter! There is freedom from condemnation; fullness and freeness of access to God; joy amid tribulations; a spiritual mind and disposition—a boon which we all so earnestly desire, for sins of the mind and disposition seem to be the last over which we get victory. There is a glorious knowledge of sonship and heirship; and, finally, the assurance of no separation from the love of God which is in Christ Jesus our Lord.

Do we not cry out with strong desire for such a life as this? The secret of it all lies in the Holy Spirit. No less than sixteen times the Holy Spirit is mentioned in Romans 8. It is the Spirit's work to war against the lusts of the flesh (Romans 8:2–3; Galatians 5:16–17). The way to overcome that "law in my members, . . . bringing me into captivity to the law of sin which is in my members" (Romans 7:23) is to lay hold of the great truth that "the law of the Spirit of life in Christ Jesus has made me free from the law of sin and death" (8:2), which was in my members working defeat and leading me to cry out, "O wretched man that I am! Who will deliver me from this body of death?" (7:24).

With the filling of the Spirit comes a deeper and more satisfying knowledge of the Word of God (John 16:13–15). The same Holy Spirit who inspired holy men of old to write the Scriptures (2 Peter 1:20–21) must also illumine the saints of today to read and understand the same Scriptures. "The natural man does not receive the things of the Spirit of God, for they are foolishness to him; nor can he know them, because they are spiritually discerned. . . . But God has revealed them to us through His Spirit" (1 Corinthians 2:14, 10). The natural understanding is darkened (Ephesians 4:18) and needs the illuminating power of the Holy Spirit before one can see the things of God as revealed in His Word (1:18; 1 John 2:20, 27). Would you have the Scriptures "opened unto you," until your heart burns within you

(Luke 24:32)? Then pray that you may be filled with the Holy Spirit of God.

The fullness of the Holy Spirit assures the believer of guidance in all the affairs of life. The Christian is "led by the Spirit of God" (Romans 8:14; Galatians 5:18). How full the book of Acts is of the guidance afforded God's children by the Holy Spirit! The believer is thus guided as to what he should say; where he should go; to whom he should speak; in what field he should labor, etc. (Acts 8:29; 10:19–20; 11:12; 16:6–7).

How often in life's journey the child of God comes to the fork of the roads, and hesitates because he knows not which way to turn! What great issues oftentimes depend upon the decision of just such moments! Which road shall we take? He who is filled with the Spirit of God will hear, at such times, a voice within, or will get some very definite and clear word from the Bible, saying, "This is the way, walk in it" (Isaiah 30:21). The indication of the Spirit's guidance may not come to you in exactly the same way it has come to others, but you will assuredly recognize the leading as being yours, and you will follow on to find that you were led aright.

THE RELATION OF THE HOLY SPIRIT TO THE WORLD

Probably there is no more vital aspect of the work of the Holy Spirit than preparing the world of the spiritually lost. It is He who first leads the soul into the light of the knowledge of God as revealed in the face of Jesus Christ.

The Holy Spirit reveals Christ to the world.
"No one can say that Jesus is Lord except by the Holy Spirit" (1 Corinthians 12:3).

The teaching of Jesus Himself with respect to this particular point is clearly set forth in His farewell discourse to the disciples: "And when He [the Holy Spirit] has come, He will convict the world of sin, and of righteousness, and of judgment: of sin, because they do not believe in Me; of righteousness, because I go to My Father, and you see Me no more; of judgment, because the ruler of this world is judged" (John 16:8–11).

It is the specific work of the Holy Spirit to take the words, deeds, and claims of Jesus to be the Savior of the world, together with the Resurrection as the proof of the genuineness of all these claims, as well as the outpouring of the Holy Spirit on the day of Pentecost—it is the work of the Holy Spirit, and He alone, to cause man to see all these things. By presenting such proof and evidence of the reality of Christ's claims and work, the Holy Spirit leaves the person who rejects Christ without excuse, and leaves the person who accepts the evidence and receives Jesus, saved.

Thus it is that men are regenerated or born again (John 3:3–5). The Holy Spirit is the agent in that regeneration of the soul of man without which no man

127

will see, much less enter, the kingdom of heaven. Our salvation is "through the washing of regeneration and renewing of the Holy Spirit" (Titus 3:5).

As men listen to the preaching of the gospel and believe it, or read the inspired Word of God and receive its testimony concerning Christ and His redemptive work, the Holy Spirit falls upon their hearts and regenerates them through that Word and that faith (James 1:18; 1 Peter 1:23; John 1:12; 3:5).

Herein lies the necessity on the part of the Christian worker to realize that the conversion of men is brought about "not by might nor by power" that is human, "but by My Spirit" (Zechariah 4:6). We may scatter the flowers of poetry; we may diffuse the light of science; we may marshal words and phrases; we may present logical arguments, elaborately stated and eloquently discussed; we may roll the thunders of eloquence and display the powers of illustration. However, none of these can save a soul unless the Holy Spirit of God falls with power on the consecrated effort we have put forth. Dead souls cannot be argued, entertained, or dazzled into life. The Holy Spirit of God must breathe life into them. Nothing but the Breath of God can make these dry bones live (see Ezekiel 37:1–14).

It is the work of the Holy Spirit to produce in the heart of man the faith that saves.

"No one can say that Jesus is Lord except by the Holy Spirit" (1 Corinthians 12:3).

It is not enough that a man be convinced by the evidence of the Word of God that Jesus Christ is not only the divinely appointed Redeemer but also his own personal Savior. Knowledge does not save. Not believing *about* but believing *into* Jesus saves a man. A man must not only believe the claims of Jesus, but must also receive Him to be all He claims to be. This is the truth of John 1:12, "But as many as received Him, to them He gave the right to become children of God, to those who believe in His name."

The power to "receive" Christ as Savior is not of ourselves, but of God's Holy Spirit. Indeed, the whole work of salvation from start to finish is of God: "For by grace you have been saved through faith, and that not of yourselves; it"—your whole salvation from start to finish—"is the gift of God" (Ephesians 2:8).

O to grace how great a debtor
Daily I'm constrained to be!

CHAPTER SEVEN

SATAN

WITHIN THE CHRISTIAN faith, probably no doctrine receives such light views as that concerning Satan. To mention the name of the devil is to invite sarcasm and ridicule, and bring forth the response, "Oh, nobody believes in the devil nowadays." Yet Satan is the adversary of both God and man. Why is such an attitude, then, common?

The caricatures of Satan as found in literature outside of the Bible, such as Milton's *Paradise Lost*, for example, are responsible to a very large extent for such unbelief in the existence and personality of Satan. The pictures of the devil in a red suit with pitchfork also make him seem a fable to many. But no earnest and devout student of the Scriptures can have a real or lasting doubt that such a being exists. This light view among believers is probably one of the cleverest schemes of the devil to obtain mastery over man. If Satan does not exist, then what is the use of man preparing himself in any way to resist the machinations of such a being as "the Evil One"?

But Satan cannot be laughed out of existence.

THE NATURE OF SATAN

Satan is a person.
"'He was a murderer from the beginning. . . . He is a liar and the father of it'" (John 8:44).

It is quite common in some quarters to speak of Satan as devil with the "d" dropped off—"evil"—thus denying the personality of the Evil One. We should not forget, however, in this connection that the word *Satan* is in the masculine, and masculine pronouns are used in speaking of him. "You are of your father the devil, and the desires of your father you want to do. He was a murderer from the beginning, and does not stand in the truth, because there is no truth in him. When he speaks a lie, he speaks from his own resources, for he is a liar and the father of it" (John 8:44). The devil lies, sins, and murders—can a mere influence do these things?

A careful and unprejudiced reading of the account of the temptation of Christ in Matthew 4:1–11 will undoubtedly impress one with the fact that Satan is just as much a person as is Christ. The same is true with regard to the story of Job, his integrity and trials, as found in Job 2–3.

The Scriptures record attributes and qualities of personality of Satan, another proof that Satan is a person (see, for instance, 1 Chronicles 21:1; Zechariah 3:1). Someone has said, "Such offices as those ascribed to Satan in the Scriptures require an officer; such a work manifests a worker; such power implies an agent; such thought proves a thinker; such designs form a personality."

Let us take, for example, the temptations of life that come to us all at some time. They are said to come from three sources: the world, the flesh, and the devil. We have no doubt that some of the temptations that beset us have their origin in the flesh, and that certain others have their promptings from a sinful environment. There are temptations in life, however, which we cannot honestly and fairly trace to either of these two sources; they must come from a personality of evil altogether outside of ourselves and our environment. It was the late Dr. Joseph Parker, of London, who said, "The old serpent, the devil, has spoken with fatal eloquence to every one of us no doubt; and I do not need a dissertation from the naturalist on the construction of a serpent's mouth to prove it. Object to the figure, if you will, but the grim, damning fact remains."

That Christ recognized the existence and activity of such a personality of evil is clearly evident from a careful reading of the gospel story (for instance, see Matthew 13:19, 39; John 13:2).

The origin of Satan was in heaven, from whence he fell, probably through pride.
"How you are fallen from heaven, O Lucifer, son of the morning! . . . For you have said in your heart: . . . 'I will exalt my throne above the stars of heaven'" (Isaiah 14:12–13).

The origin of Satan is not clearly stated in the Scriptures. It is inferred from certain Scriptures (such as Isaiah 14:12–14; Ezekiel 28:14–19; 2 Corinthians 11:14; 1 Timothy 3:6; Jude 6) that he was once an angel of light, probably the leader of all the shining hosts of God, and that, somehow or other, probably through pride, he and other angels fell from their glorious estate and were cast down from their places in heaven. That, to some extent at least, Satan still retains some of that former dignity, power, and might may be inferred from Jude 8 and 9: Referring to those false teachers who "speak evil of dignitaries," Jude wrote, "Yet Michael the archangel, in contending with the devil, when he disputed about the body of Moses, dared not bring against him a reviling accusation, but said, 'The Lord rebuke you!'" What great power, think you, does Satan still retain, when Christ referred to him as the "strong man, fully armed" (Luke 11:21), and "the ruler of this world" (John 14:30)?

Nor is the teaching of Paul less clear and distinct than that of Christ. To Paul, Satan is the "prince of the power of the air, the spirit who now works in the sons of disobedience" (Ephesians 2:2). Is there not a tremendous supernatural force of "principalities [and] powers" subject to his word and will—"his angels" as they are called (6:11–12; cf. Matthew 25:41 KJV)? Who is "the god of this world"? To whom do the men of the world bow and whom do they serve? Is it not Satan (2 Corinthians 4:4; 1 John 5:19 KJV)? Undoubtedly so. To the great apostle, the kingdom of darkness, over which Satan and his hosts presided, was as stern a reality as the kingdom of light over which Christ and His good angels ruled. Paul felt it his life work to turn people from the power of Satan unto the power of God (Acts 26:18).

THE NAMES OF SATAN

Satan is called the adversary.
"Your adversary the devil walks about like a roaring lion" (1 Peter 5:8).
"Satan standing . . . to oppose him" (Zechariah 3:1).

The name "Satan" means "an adversary"; in 1 Peter 5:8, he is referred to as "your adversary the devil." By this designation we are to understand that Satan is the perpetual and uncompromising foe, the adversary of man, continually opposing him in every work of righteousness which he seeks to accomplish. Of course, in the same sense, Satan is equally the adversary of God, for the purposes of God and the children of God are of the same nature.

Satan is called the accuser.
"Then I heard a loud voice saying in heaven, 'Now salvation, and strength, and the kingdom of our God, and the power of His Christ have come, for the *accuser* of our brethren, who accused them before our God day and night, has been cast down'" (Revelation 12:10).

Satan is the "accuser of the brethren," the *diabolos*, the one who slanders God to man (Genesis 3:1–7) and man to God (Job 1:9–11; 2:4–5). Herein lies our need of "an Advocate with the Father, Jesus Christ the righteous" (1 John 2:1). Satan is always on the lookout for the faults and failings of the people of God in order that, magnifying them, he may, misrepresenting the saints, bring their faults and sins before God.

No scheme, device, or plan is too wicked for him to resort to if he can thwart the purpose of God or spoil the plan of God in a believer's life. For this reason he is called "the Wicked One" or "the Evil One" (Matthew 13:19; 1 John 5:18–19). And every such plan in the heart of any person, believer or unbeliever, to hurt, injure, or destroy the child of God or hurt his influence or reputation has its origin with the devil; he "put it into the heart" (John 13:2, 27; Acts 5:3).

Satan is called the tempter.
"The tempter came to Him" (Matthew 4:3).

It is principally as "the tempter" that Satan is described in the Scriptures (Matthew 4:3). And as such, not one of the children of men is able to escape his malicious scheming. God had one Son without sin, but no son without temptation. Even Jesus Himself was "tempted by the devil" (Matthew 4:1). And how cunning and sagacious is the tempter at such times!

How we need to be on our guard against "the wiles of the devil," his carefully laid plots and plans to overthrow us or to cause us to fall! To accomplish such he appears to us as "an angel of light" (2 Corinthians 11:14), as one who would help our faith (Matthew 4:6). The "old serpent" is subtle (Genesis 3:1), and, as the "roaring lion" (1 Peter 5:8), he is strong. Satan's subtlety is seen in tempting us in our weak moments, as he did Christ in the wilderness (Matthew 4) and in the Garden of Gethsemane (Luke 22), and Elijah, in the reaction that came from his great victory over the prophets of Baal (1 Kings 19). When we are strong and after great successes, we need to be on our guard against the temptations of the devil (Matthew 4:1; John 6:15; cf. verses 1–14).

How many a man, who would shun the thing that is clearly and openly wrong, may be tempted as was Christ to do right things in a wrong way, to bring about good results by questionable methods (Matthew

4:1–11). How often does Satan delude his followers by giving them power to perform "signs and lying wonders" (2 Thessalonians 2:9). The fact that any man or religious cult is able to perform healings is no sign that he or it is of God; that power may be given by the devil.

RESPONDING TO SATAN

We must exercise our victory over Satan.
"The ruler of this world is judged" (John 16:11).

Satan is a conquered enemy. The death of Christ on the cross did something to Satan; there, potentially at least, Satan and his authority over men received their death-stroke. "'Now is the judgment of this world; now the ruler of this world will be cast out. And I, if I am lifted up from the earth, will draw all peoples to Myself'" (John 12:31–32). "You have overcome the wicked one" (1 John 2:14). Jesus Christ, by His atoning death and resurrection from the dead, made Satan a conquered enemy so far as the believer in Christ is concerned. At Calvary our Savior despoiled the principalities and the powers and "made a public spectacle, . . . triumphing over them" by His cross (Colossians 2:15).

Satan can touch the child of God only as he is allowed to by the Father: "And the Lord said to Satan, 'Behold, all that he has is in your power; only do not lay a hand on his person'" (Job 1:12). Jesus said to His disciples, and to us through them, "Be of good cheer, I have overcome the world" (John 16:33). Christ in the heart of the believer is greater than all the power of the devil in the world (cf. 1 John 4:4).

In our endeavor to lead victorious lives, it is exceedingly important that we really understand exactly what has taken place with reference to Satan and his power because of the finished redemptive work of Jesus Christ. Victory is already achieved for us through Christ. We are under no obligation to yield to temptation. We do not need to sin (1 John 2:1). The place of Satan is under the feet of the believer: "And the God of peace will crush Satan under your feet shortly" (Romans 16:20).

Satan must be resisted:
"Resist the devil and he will flee from you" (James 4:7).

Peter warns us to "be sober, be vigilant; because your adversary the devil walks about like a roaring lion, seeking whom he may devour." Our strategy must be to "resist him, steadfast in the faith" (1 Peter 5:8–9).

In order to resist, we must stand clad, not in any armor of our own making, but in the armor of God so completely described in Ephesians 6:10–20. *Obedience and loving submission to the will of God* (James 4:7) is also a secret of victory over the wiles of the devil. To *store the Word of God in the heart* (as Christ undoubtedly had done, judging from His ready use of it in the wilderness temptation) is to be always ready for the sudden and vicious attacks of the adversary of the soul (Ephesians 6:17).

Someday there will be no adversary of the soul of man roaming around seeking whom he may devour. In the plan of God for the ages there will be a time when Satan shall be cast into the lake of fire, there to be "tormented day and night forever and ever" (Revelation 20:10).

Satan has a purpose in the world and a place in the divine plan. Have you ever stood outside a blacksmith's shop and watched the blacksmith and his helper? The smith takes a piece of red- or white-hot iron out of the fire and places it on the anvil. Holding the bit of iron by the pinchers in one hand, he places it just where he wants it on the anvil. In the other hand he holds a small hammer or other steel implement with which to mould the hot iron into whatever shape he desires. At his side stands the helper, a great big, burly fellow, stripped to the waist, with a huge sledgehammer in his hand, waiting for orders from the blacksmith. When the signal is given the helper swings the great hammer, using all his main strength until he is a mass of perspiration, in shaping that bit of iron in the smith's hand into whatever shape the blacksmith himself desires.

So it is with Satan. God holds His children in His own hand, and He makes the devil sweat to make saints out of them, according to His own will.